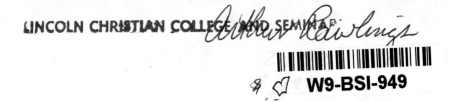

How to Break
Growth Barriers

This book is a must. . . . Penetrating insights that are both spiritual and pragmatic.
            —*Bill Bright*
            President, Campus Crusade for Christ International

Carl George's best book to date . . . practical, relevant, and inspirational.
            —*Rick Warren*
            Pastor, Saddleback Valley Community Church,
            Mission Viejo, Calif.

A momentous book that will become the textbook in breaking growth barriers.
            —Dale Galloway
            Pastor, New Hope Community Church, Portland, Oreg.

The disarming thing about Carl George is how he blends the science of Church Growth (if there is such a thing) with the spirit of Church Growth (and there *is* such a thing). That "spirit" is the Holy Spirit, and I'm grateful for Carl's emphasis as we seek ways to partner with the Savior who is building His church so wondrously today.
            —Jack Hayford
            Pastor, Church on the Way, Van Nuys, Calif.

I particularly like Carl George's emphasis on the ministry of all people. In this, he stands in the line of Martin Luther and Elton Trueblood.
            —Kenneth C. Haugk
            Founder and Executive Director, Stephen Ministries

The author has offered compelling reasons why care givers must find a new way of caring. The needs are too great and the world is too complex to go on with business as usual.
            —Bill Hinson
            First United Methodist Church, Houston, Tex.

The book commands "must read" status for all who do ministry and teach others to do ministry. Carl George has taken a hard look at the major problem facing the church today. His solutions help us do the work of God in the most effective way possible.
            —John W. Reed
            Chairman, Pastoral Ministries Department,
            Dallas Theological Seminary

Carl George is both prophetic and practical. His latest book is a great toolbox for leaders living on the cutting edge.
            —Walt Kallestad
            Community Church of Joy ELCA, Glendale, Ariz.

How to Break Growth Barriers

*Capturing Overlooked
Opportunities
for Church Growth*

Carl F. George
with
Warren Bird

BAKER BOOK HOUSE
Grand Rapids, Michigan 49516

© 1993 by Carl F. George
Published by Baker Book House
P. O. Box 6287, Grand Rapids, MI 49516-6287

Library of Congress Cataloging-in Publication Data

George, Carl F.
    How to break growth barriers : Capturing overlooked opportunities for church growth
Carl F. George with Warren Bird.
      p. cm.
    Includes bibliographical references and index.
    ISBN 0-8010-3853-7
    1. Pastoral theology. 2. Church growth. I. Bird, Warren.
II. Title.
BV4011.G43   1993
253—dc20   92-32709

Other books by Carl F. George:
Prepare Your Church for the Future (Revell, 1991)

By Carl F. George and Robert E. Logan:
Leading and Managing Your Church (Revell, 1987)

By C. Peter Wagner (ed.) and Carl F. George (contributor)
Church Growth: The State of the Art (Tyndale, 1986)

Contents

95946

List of Figures

Foreword

Pastors and laypersons alike want their church to grow. And, as author Carl George believes, so does God!

The following pages present far more than a manual for church growth. It offers an amazing stimulus for effective ministry and outreach through that body of believers of which our Lord Jesus Christ has said, "I will build my church" (Matt. 16:18).

The Word of God indicates that God himself has ordained only three institutions for the welfare of humanity—governments, the family, and the church. All three are under severe attack by the enemy.

Carl George recognizes the church as the vital force for good and righteousness in these significant days. No institution is more important or more needed in our communities, nation, and world than the church (as abused and denigrated as it is in far too many circles).

Few individuals in America are more knowledgeable concerning the church than my friend Carl George, director of the Charles E. Fuller Institute of Evangelism and Church Growth. Few have counseled as wide a range of pastors and church leaders as he. A good physician, he offers helpful, practical prescriptions, both spiritual and numerical, for a church that needs resuscitation.

If we as individuals, and the church corporately, are to be salt and light as Jesus has indicated (*see* Matt. 5:13), the wise counsel and advice in these pages will provide spiritual perspectives for this continuing process. Scriptures give clear guidelines and Carl George helpfully applies these to churches soon facing the twenty-first century.

This is not a book without challenge. If growth barriers are to be broken, there must be pain. Carl George shows great sensitivity to the world that pastors and lay leaders face each week, but he also offers much hope in how to become an overcomer.

The wise counsel found in these pages will be of inestimable value to everyone who loves and seeks to serve the church.

I am convinced that any church leader worthy of the title will gain an enlarged vision for what God wants to do through your church as a result of applying the biblical principles in the pages that follow.

Watch for the models of the rancher and the sheepherder. Ask yourself: "Where do I fit in this arena?" And, no matter where your barriers seem to be—50, 200, 400, 800, or 5,000—you will find valuable, readily applicable help.

Let's break down these barriers, to the glory of God. It *can* be done! Here's a plan to make it happen.

Ted W. Engstrom
President Emeritus
World Vision

Acknowledgments

This book is dedicated to those pastors, lay leaders, and church and mission executives with whom I have had the privilege of working over the years through various consultations, seminars, and convocations. You have influenced, impressed, and taught me in more ways than this page could possibly express.

It takes a great deal of courage to face the pain that accompanies change, for in the breaking of every barrier there must be the willingness, akin to that of an Olympic athlete, to press the limits of personal endurance. Without such risk, a person remains within borders that are too calm to be challenging.

None of us has approached the issue of church growth without an armful of experiences, biases, and dreams. Our questions are not What would be ideal? but What is undone, which, if done, would make a difference?

In that quest for hardiness, for the will to implement what we know as wisdom, I could not have written this book without the example of the many "championship players" who are making a significant contribution to the well-being of others, including myself.

Many thanks also to all who read the manuscript at various stages and offered both encouragement and valuable critique: Alex Aronis, Lamar Austin, David Bartels, Michelle Bird, Robert Brady, Jr., Claude Florent, Ray DuPont, Brian Chronister, H. Robert Cowles, Mike Cunningham, Sam Downing, Mark Edwards, Marcia Gautier, Grace George, James Hobby, Jr., Sharon Houghton, David Hricik, Louis Huesmann, Arnie Mickelson, Joey Johnson, Jim and Barbara Nelson, John W. Reed, Hal Seed, Shirley Shively, Terry Smith, and Bob Wido.

My thanks as well to the artists and computer graphics specialists who refined the charts: Tim Allen, Karan Banando, Val O'Barr, Diane Swatrz, and Mike Wilson.

Finally, whenever charts or other visuals are used in a book, questions inevitably arise from readers who want to understand more about how copyright law applies to their particular situation. Here is how the permission issues works for *How to Break Growth Barriers.* Individuals purchasing this book are allowed to reproduce the graphics for not-for-profit uses in a local church. Quotations from the text, of up to 150 words, may be used without special authorization in reviews, bulletin inserts, seminar notebooks, overhead transparencies, and other printed media.

Otherwise, written permission from the copyright holder (the author) *is necessary* to reproduce the charts, or any other parts of this book, in films, videotapes, books, magazines, denominational publications, or any other form. For further information, please contact the author at P. O. Box 5407, Diamond Bar, CA 91765. Phone: 714-861-5253.

Foreign-language translations are likewise prohibited under international copyright law to protect the integrity of the book's content. To obtain written permission for translation and assistance in contextualizing the content, contact

Baker Book House
P.O. Box 6287
Grand Rapids, MI 49516-6287
Phone: 616-676-9185

PART 1

Identify
Your Vision

1

What Can This Book Do for You?

Go with me to a country just hit by a devastating earthquake, where 45,000 people are injured or dead. Two medical teams, each headed by a doctor, are being airlifted to the heart of the disaster area.

The physician leading the first crew steps out of the helicopter and is immediately overwhelmed by all the carnage he sees. There, barely ten paces away, workers are pulling a mangled living body from under the rubble.

Moved by compassion, the doctor rushes over and calculates the personnel, equipment, and facilities needed to help this victim. He assigns half his medical team and half their supplies to work on this one person.

A handful of survivors, sensing the availability of help, bring the physician another case. This victim is in even worse condition. The doctor assigns the rest of his medical team and resources to care for this person.

Now the doctor faces a worse dilemma than when his helicopter touched down. He would like to treat 44,998 more people but has already expended all his resources on the first two bodies presented to him.

The only solution, he decides, is to make himself even more available. He resolves that he and his staff will push themselves harder. They will be on call twenty hours a day, seven days a week, to treat as many individuals as possible.

Unfortunately, a few weeks later this well-intentioned medic is forced to return home. His body has not kept pace with his desire to help. With his resistance lowered he has caught one of the diseases rampant in the disaster area. The care he and his team have provided must come to a standstill until a replacement arrives.

Meanwhile, what is the second medical team doing? Their preliminary assessment, likewise, takes only a matter of moments. They, too, are deeply shocked and moved with compassion toward the massive death and pain evident in every direction. They see widespread malnutrition, open wounds, and other horrible conditions.

People are suffering and dying before their eyes.

The physician heading this second unit quickly concludes that her small group by itself is inadequate. So, instead of scooping up the first person in sight and immediately beginning treatment, this doctor opts for a different plan. She tries to calculate a strategy that will touch a maximum number of people in the least amount of time, using the scarce resources available.

The doctor announces to her team, "Let's train some people as life-support engineers." One group will make sure safe drinking water is available, another will deal with shelter issues, another with food. Yet another group will work on waste control and public health by repairing the city-wide sewer system to take the fecal matter off the streets before it mixes into the water supply or spreads into the homes.

This relief and preventative care, multiplied throughout the disaster area, will retard the growth of infection and allow the medical intervention to have a greater impact.

Having mapped out a program to provide the essentials of survival and reduce infectious agents, the doctor next addresses issues of proper nutrition and other preventable forms of need.

In the meantime, her medical team begins training the healthier survivors to serve as health officers. Their focus is on remedial and interventionary care, starting with the people who, if treated, have a good prognosis for recovery.

Everyone in the disaster area is keenly aware that a very practical reason exists for giving priority to those who are getting well. The need is of such tremendous proportions that every additional able-bodied worker can help make a significant difference.

Which Team Would You Choose?

Suppose you as a typical North American pastor or Christian leader were to watch the above-described scenario and be asked which of the medical teams was more caring. Which would you choose? Remember, both teams had equally strong feelings of love and compassion. They differed only in how they showed their concern.

The initial response of most Christians, including trained leaders, is to choose to act like the first group. They want to help, they allow their impulsiveness to plunge them into immediate action, and their compassion focuses their attention on the most urgent needs.

However, I suggest and will affirm this underlying principle throughout this book: An emphasis on leadership development illustrated by the second above group paves the way for a higher level of long-range care. A systems-based, managerial approach, when prayerfully operated in dependence on the Holy Spirit, is the most effective way to deliver the most widespread continuing infusion of desperately needed care. It also models most closely the way Jesus worked with his twelve disciples.

Unfortunately, like the first doctor in this example, many of us fail to recognize what can happen when a crisis is of such tremendous scope. The field of need is too big for us. We frantically work twenty hours a day, only to come down with spiritual chronic-fatigue syndrome. Worse, our underlying motivation will stem from a mistaken assumption. We wrongly suppose that the key to effective ministry is our personal availability.

That is, most pastors frame their priorities around a supposition that widespread ministry will occur only when they are active as primary care givers.

> We wrongly suppose that the key to effective
> ministry is our personal availability.

I propose this alternative: The more fundamental need is for church leaders to craft a systemic[1] approach to pastoral care. To the extent that caregivers in a local church* become so preoccupied with the nearest bleeding body that they cannot keep the whole system alive, they will allow whole sections of their church to perish in the process. They must, rather, attend to the big picture.

Pastors and lay leaders must see with eyes of faith to catch a glimpse of a bigger view of their church's ministry. They cannot continue to accept the first case to cross their path, wrap their lives around it, and allow the rest of the world to go down the tubes. Rather, they must allocate their resources as strategically as a medical emergency team triages a crisis. Nor do they demonstrate wise leadership if they provide all the ministry themselves, even if they do discover how to clock in a twenty-five-hour day.

Many people's lives are devastated. They need continuing large doses of prayer, ongoing care, and special attention. The church will want to make sure the help they need is available to them. But other people require just a little assistance, and then they can help with the ministering.

Yes, it is heartrending to bypass one needy person to give attention to another. Yes, such choices will receive recriminations by certain well-intentioned church people. But church leaders who want to maximize their impact must develop a means of budgeting their energies.

---

*Throughout this book I use the word *church* to indicate a local body of believers (Bronx Christian Alliance Church) or the sum of all churches (the church as the body of Christ). The word *church* always refers to people, not their place of worship—which I term *church building* or *church facility*.

The word *congregation* in this book is not synonymous with *church*. *Congregation*, rather, will signify a certain middle-sized group, which is bigger than a home-based cell group and smaller than a church-wide worship celebration.

Peter Wagner, in *Your Church Can Grow*[2], first popularized the nomenclature of *cell*, *congregation*, and *celebration*. My book *Prepare Your Church for the Future*[3] develops the implications of each particular size gathering.

Remember, however, the need on which this master plan is built. In no way does it stem from a lack of mercy. Rather, the leader's prayerful goal is to determine how to apply his or her time and energy so that the most people can receive the best possible care in the shortest amount of time with the best use of the resources.

Ultimately, this multiplication strategy, when guided and empowered by the Holy Spirit, will result in the most people being touched. In addition, sometimes a leader's best personal growth occurs while he or she learns to train others for leadership.

Why This Book Is Relevant to You

This book is designed to help you, a church leader, enlarge your vision for what God wants to do through your church. It will also coach you in the leadership perspective and skills necessary to break through whatever current growth barrier you face.

To begin, chapters 2 and 3 will help you identify the vision God has for your church, as well as the vision you currently convey to your people. You will also gain insight into how to develop a more listening-sensitive life, and how to increase your "visionizing" abilities.

Chapter 4 will help you see your church as a system so as to better know if it is or is not growing. You will finish this chapter with a better handle on the importance of accurately diagnosing your particular church situation.

Chapter 5 deals with the motive issue: Why should you want your church to grow? What are some unhealthy factors that can lie behind a growth momentum? Does God necessarily call every church to numerical growth?

The heart of the book, chapters 6 and 7, presents the rancher and sheepherder styles of ministry, explains why the sheepherder mentality is usually a fundamental obstacle to most church growth, and offers you guidance to assess your leadership gifts and style.

Then come several illustrations of what ranching could look like in your ministry (chapter 8), especially as it relates to certain conflicts in the church. You will also understand how the current codependency and recovery movement is linked to the sheepherder's dilemma.

The rest of the book shows how to break specific growth barriers. What are the keys to breaking the 200 barrier (chapter 9), the 400 barrier (chapter 10), and the 800 barrier (chapter 11)?

The final chapter (chapter 12) points you to the ministry paradigm of the future. It explains why certain churches experience phenomenal conversion growth and wholehearted discipleship. It shows how to build these essential components into your church right now so as to lay the foundation for unimpeded growth in the future.

Maybe Your Situation Is Different

Whatever size church you now serve, chances are that numerous growth opportunities are present but overlooked. After fifteen years of consulting across dozens of denominations, I have yet to be in a church where more growth opportunity is not present than the church is willing to respond to.

Church growth is like planted grass. If you stand on the seeded bed, the new green shoots do not have a chance. Give them water and light, and they will grow naturally.

Does that analogy seem too simplistic? I believe it describes what God wants to do for his church. He wants to build it in such a way that not even the gates of hell can block its expansion (Matt. 16:18).

Could it be that we are so accustomed to working with bonsai trees that we have lost sight of and hope for ongoing, unstunted growth? Could we church leaders, like a dynasty of oriental gardeners, be part of an ongoing tradition that twists, bruises, pinches, and clips the roots of our churches so as to prevent their being overtaken by growth? Maybe, despite our intentions otherwise, we do so without even realizing it.

Barriers to growth can usually be resolved. The key issue at your church is probably not a stubborn deacon or even a perennially unmet church budget. Instead, it is probably the lack of a workable plan to overcome certain obstacles in ministry. As the newspaper-comic Pogo has said, "We have met the enemy, and he is us."

The first person to deal with in the chain of change is the minister, because he or she sets a pace that either assures nongrowth or permits growth.

Are You a Sheepherder or a Rancher?

As with the medical teams described earlier, the needs around you are of such tremendous proportions that all systems of care can be completely overwhelmed. Hurting people are in such abundance that they can almost drive you to despair.

The typical response to widespread need is what this book will call sheepherding. This style of caring makes the pastor available as the primary care giver to everyone who will respond.

By contrast, just as the more realistic and practical scenario for the second doctor in the earthquake zone was to teach people mutual self-care, you, too, must attend to the management dimension. This style of caring is what I will call ranching.[4]

To become a rancher you learn to do more than offer empathetic responses to human need. You also acknowledge certain realities: You cannot deliver help to all people at the levels they require. Instead, you must take a more managerial, conceptual view of things (as explained in chapters 6 through 8), which in the long run is not only most loving but is the perspective Jesus exemplified.

In short, I suggest a changed paradigm for church leadership. You must shift from doing the caring, which usually means you do it yourself, to seeing to it that people get cared for, which means you develop and manage a system of care giving that will include as many of your church's lay leaders as possible (see Figure 1).

The principles in this book do not require that you abandon your care giving skills. Rather, they will urge you to adopt a new perspective on sheepherding by asking to whom you should make yourself available as a primary care giver and how you can best allocate the time and energy you put into hands-on ministry.

This ranching outlook is taught by a number of church-growth analysts. Although their terminology may vary, a unifying theme runs through each of the following writers:

> Growth, evangelism and the expansion of the church depend as much on a leader's ability to develop an expansive infrastructure as on any other factor except prayer. . . . The church that grows beyond the 200 barrier is the church that decides to minister to its people in a comprehensive organization rather than a family-type fellowship.
>
> (Bill M. Sullivan, *Ten Steps to Breaking the 200 Barrier*)[5]

Figure 1

Are You *One* Care Giver?

or
a Maker of Care Givers?

© 1992 Carl F. George

There is very persuasive evidence that suggests that: (1) the normal historical pressures on the pastor, especially in smaller congregations and in new missions, tend to cause him to accept a shepherd role; (2) if the pastor of a new mission accepts the shepherd role in the early years of the new mission, attendance probably will level off at an average of less than one hundred. . . ; (3) the churches that continue to increase in size year after year tend to have rancher-style ministers as their pastors; (4) small congregations and many of the congregations that are declining in size tend to have shepherd-style pastors; and (5) after a congregation has experienced being served by a shepherd-style minister the members often resist, oppose, or resent a minister who seeks to function in a rancher-style role.

In simple language it appears that one reason approximately one-half of all the congregations in American Protestantism average fewer than 75 at the principle weekly worship service is the combination of the traditional image of the role of the pastor with the normal institutional and personal pressures that cause the minister to function as a shepherd. . . . The shepherd role . . . tends to inhibit the evangelistic outreach of those congregations.

(Lyle E. Schaller, *Survival Tactics in the Parish*)[6]

Two leadership style shifts are required for breaking the "125 Barrier." Shift #1: The pastor must shift from establishing deep one-to-one relationships to establishing group relationship. . . . Shift #2: The pastor must shift from being a foreman to being a supervisor. An effective supervisor delegates responsibility. . . . Growing past the "125 barrier" requires a shift from "doing it all yourself" to "getting others involved."

(Harry H. Fowler, *Breaking Barriers of New Church Growth*)[7]

Church growth cannot be sustained unless the laity are mobilized to fulfill their distinctive ministries both in the church and in the world. . . .

In a small church of up to say 65, the management style of the leader will probably be at the level of foreman. . . . He is available to be personally involved in every task which comes to hand.

In churches with a membership of between 66 and 150, the most frequently encountered leadership level is that of supervisor. . . . He is on hand to deal with an emergency and resolve any difficulties which may arise. Church ministers who operate in this way have their phones constantly ringing, or find people forever at the door. . . .

The leader has to change his management style to middle management level to get far into the 151-450 member bracket. Middle management involves delegation with accountability. When people are
invited to undertake some responsibilities in the church, they are
given appropriate decision-making power. . . .
The church with more than 450 members . . . needs top-level management skills to weld his professional team together. . . .
When a church tops the 1,000 membership mark, . . . the presiding
minister . . . functions as chairman of the board. He dreams his
dreams, formulates his plans, and excites others with the vision of
his perceptions of where the church could be five years hence.

(Eddie Gibbs, *I Believe in Church Growth*)[8]

The most formidable obstacle to growth that I know of is a pastor
who thinks negatively and who is pessimistic about growth opportunities in the community. Such a pastor generally feels that the basic
task of the church is to care for those sheep already in the fold rather
than to concentrate on winning lost sheep and constantly incorporat-
ing new ones into the flock. . . .
If the first vital sign of a growing church is a pastor who is using
God-given gifts to lead the church into growth, the second is a well-
mobilized laity. . . .
In a smaller church of up to 200 members the pastor can do all the
work, and many do. But such a church will not be able to grow past
that point without lay ministry.
Pastors of growing churches, whether they be large or small, know
how to motivate their laypeople, how to create structures which permit them to be active and productive, and how to guide them into
meaningful avenues of Christian service.

(Peter Wagner, *Your Church Can Grow*)[9]

No church can grow beyond the ability of the pastoral leader to delegate responsibilities to staff and lay ministers. . . . Lay ministers
must become a mobilized force in the church if significant growth is
to occur. . . . The pastor in a growing church is always a central figure, but he is careful to surround himself with gifted, responsible,
work-oriented laypersons who function as lay ministers.

(Charles Chaney and Ron Lewis, *Design for Church Growth*)[10]

Growth occurs when Christ is recognized as the Chief Shepherd, . . . when the undershepherds [pastors] adequately provide for the sheep, ... and when the sheep follow the shepherds. . . . An additional issue that is being brought to light today by church-growth thinkers is the maximum size of the flock. Just how many sheep can one shepherd know, feed, love, protect, and direct? New Testament evidence abounds that a plurality of elders existed in cities where churches were established. . . . If properly decentralized . . . lay ministers are considered the "nervous system" of the church. They show concern to the families of the church and serve as a communication line concerning illness, bereavement, and joyful occasions among the members. They also seek to encourage each member to participate fully in the church's programs. Among many churches this practical implementation of the "shepherd-sheep" concept is taking on a greater importance.

(Elmer Towns, John Vaughan, David Seifert,
The Complete Book of Church Growth)[11]

Do you see the common thread in what these growth specialists all say? An effective leader accomplishes the work through others. The task is too great for one person. It is more important for the leader of a growing church to produce other leaders than to perform personal ministry.

All pastors and lay leaders who grasp this concept and act on it will find the scope of their ministry to be broadened. Many may

> An effective leader accomplishes the work through others. The task is too great for one person.

gain insight into certain long-standing patterns of personal co-dependency (to be discussed in chapter 8). Still others will discover a delightful liberation from the "oughts" of false guilt.

The ideas in this book, which I believe are both grounded in Scripture and sensitive to what the Holy Spirit wants to do in our time, are tools that will help us evangelize and disciple our cities and towns beyond our wildest imaginations. Followup gaps will be filled. Alienation and despair will be transformed into hope, faith, and love. And broken families will be rebuilt as people are re-parented in the context of spiritual kinship groups.

My hope also is that readers will understand why Jesus urges them to focus their prayers not merely on the harvest nor on themselves as ministers but on the leadership-formation issue: that the Lord of the harvest will "send out workers into his harvest field" (Matt. 9:38).

Are you ready for such a challenge?

For Further Thought

1. Of the two medical teams described, whose vision and management style is most similar to yours? Where does the analogy break down in your situation?

2. In your church experience, would you say the sheepherder style or the rancher style is more predominant? Why? What factors influence churches to desire sheepherders or to tolerate ranchers?

3. What is the main purpose and message of this book? Which chapter appears to be most relevant for you?

4. Of the different writers quoted in this chapter, which spoke most pointedly to you?

5. Based on your knowledge of Scripture, what teachings and illustrations come to mind that support a sheepherding perspective of leadership? a ranching perspective?

6. Put check marks in front of your three areas of greatest strength. Put asterisks in front of the three that probably need the most improvement.

    a. Knowing God's vision for your church (chapter 2).

    b. Communicating vision to your church (chapter 3).

    c. Detecting vision limiters in your church (chapter 2).

    d. Practicing a prayer life that is open to vision (chapter 2).

    e. Understanding the sources of growth in your church (chapter 4).

    f. Being willing to ask God if he has a greater agenda for your church than you do (chapter 5).

    g. Viewing the rancher ministry style as a more effective disciple-making strategy than the sheepherder style (chapter 6)

h. Identifying ways that you behave like a sheepherder (chapters 6 and 7)

i. Identifying ways that you behave like a rancher (chapters 6 and 7).

j. Dealing with difficult groups in your church (chapter 8).

k. Understanding how your upbringing and personal co-dependencies affect your ministry (chapter 8).

l. Developing a specific strategy to break current numeric growth barriers (chapters 9, 10, and 11).

m. Developing a long-range plan designed to prevent your church from becoming less caring as it grows larger (chapter 12).

2

How Can You Enlarge
Your Vision?

After King David led Israel into an era of unprecedented peace, security, and wealth, he held a conversation with the prophet Nathan, which I paraphrase from 2 Samuel chapter 7.

"How do you like my new cedar-lined, state-of-the-art king's mansion?" David asked.

"Pretty nice," came Nathan's reply.

"I've been thinking about building one for God," David commented.

"Great idea. Do what's in your heart," answered Nathan.

But that night the Lord said to Nathan, "Go tell David I didn't ask for that. I'm in the business of providing houses for *him*. When did I ask him to make a home for *me*? All I want David to do is to be my servant."

The implication? It is easy to create a dream of what we could do for God without consulting him as to what he has in mind. Just because we have thought up an idea and can list ways it could bring glory to our Lord, we still have no guarantee that he has said yes.

The purpose of this chapter and the next, therefore, is to offer guidance in identifying the vision God has for your church as well as the vision that guides you at present. You will also gain insight into how to increase your vision-casting or communicating abilities and how to develop a more listening-sensitive prayer life.

What Can Vision Do?

Your ability to provide leadership to your church is directly connected to how you envision a preferred future and then effectively communicate that goal to your constituency.

Today's business world, for example, was enhanced by the vision of a man named Fred Smith. He conceived of a way to make geography irrelevant. He said, in effect, "We're going to fix it so that if Joe Customer orders a widget, we can make it possible to have that widget on Joe's desk the next morning by 10:00, no matter where in North America Joe lives."

That is precisely what happened, resulting in a new household word: Federal Express. Based on his vision, Fred Smith designed an entire system of tools, from airplane fleets to state-of-the-art computerized inventory control.

I have dialed Fed-Ex's toll-free number and, in a matter of seconds, been told something like, "Yes, the package we picked up yesterday in Los Angeles is on our truck in Watchung, New Jersey, and will be delivered to Sunshine Shampoo Company in about ten minutes." Wow! How could they know that? It happened not by accident, but because Smith prepared and executed a vision.

What Can Limit Your Vision?

I regularly listen to pastors and lay leaders as they talk about their dreams and goals. Most of them already have some kind of vision they can articulate. But in their accounts I often detect the equivalent of signposts on the highways of their imaginations. These markers, because of the restrictions they create, virtually guarantee that most churches will not achieve their full potential.

What does that mental image say? "Vision Limit, Do Not Exceed." This chapter will help you see those markers that may appear to identify full-fledged visions but have their own built-in limitations on visions of growth. It will also show you how to ask God if he has a greater agenda for your church than you do.

I have counted at least fifteen such limiting vision shapers. Each of them restrains a pastor's leadership ability and a church's growth.

1. The first vision limiter stems from a problem-solving focus. Peter Drucker, author of such books as *Managing the Non-Profit*

Organization, insists that problem solving is an important aspect of management. He points out, however, that the primary accomplishment of problem solving is to take something that is unraveled and reweave it so that it works just about as well as it did before it broke. But, Drucker says, mere problem solving fails to capitalize on emerging opportunity.[1]

Therefore, a problem-solving focus will not necessarily guide a church to grow significantly. Instead, it is more likely to help a church merely maintain its present circumstances.

Someone has said that church leaders have become keepers of the aquarium rather than fishermen of the deep. Tending the aquarium (or the flock) is an important role. No one should downplay its significance. At the same time, remember that doing so does not automatically lead to growth.

True, in some cases where a strong birth rate is present, a problem-solving focus assists a church to preserve what it has and even enlarge as a result. But in most situations, unless evangelism is present, growth cannot be sustained.

> In most situations, unless evangelism is present, growth cannot be maintained.

2. A second growth limiter occurs when a church's leadership says, "I'm busy enough now." When translated, those words usually mean, "I feel tired, and my vision of a 'preferred future' is to be less tired. If I'm this weary now, what am I going to feel like if we add a 10 percent increase to every ministry I now oversee?"

I discovered this full-calendar limit as I watched one pastor personally sign seven hundred letters for his parish's annual fund campaign. When he had done around three hundred, he looked over at me, stopped only long enough to turn the page for the next signature, and said, "With seven hundred people on my roll, I have all I can say grace over now. If you're asking me for money to help start a new work, I will gladly put it in the budget for which I am signing these letters, but please don't ask me to accept more sheep in the flock. The ones I have now are just about getting away from me."

He did possess a vision. It was to watch out for the sheep well enough so that he could live and they would feel adequately managed. There is nothing inherently wrong with these results—if the Almighty has called him to do just that much, and no more.

3. Third, some people follow a lockstep vision limit. This barrier to an enlarged harvest says, "I must make certain not to go any more slowly than my colleagues are going." In other words, "My standard is to keep up with the rest of the pack."

If you are such a leader, you are begging for fatigue. Why? Opportunities vary from church to church. The mix and fit between your personality, your time of life, the maturity level of the church you now serve, and so forth, may sharply contrast with that of your sister church across town.

Maybe their mortgage was paid off by a timely bequest, and yours was not (or vice versa). Maybe their pastoral family, with their 2.4 children, is at the perfect age and life stage for that church, and yours does not seem to be (or vice versa).

The lockstep mentality does reflect a vision of sorts. And it can drive a church's behavior. "Well, Pastor, *they're* having a successful vacation Bible school. Just look at their ad in the newspaper. Why can't we have a successful vacation Bible school?" Sometimes it works because it promotes action through envy.

The lockstep pattern can work in reverse as well. If you break step and shoot upward like a sunflower in a garden of poppies, your "friends" may want to prune you back. If your church grows and receives attention at more than one annual denominational meeting in a row, you might be abandoned by the people who were once pleasant to be around. Some of them will be caught up in jealousy and will challenge your motives, shun you, and otherwise criticize you.

In short, for you to compare yourself with the "average" church, whether it leads to your grumbling or gloating, is unproductive. Doing so will tie you into a lockstep pattern that says, "We've got to do better, because I do not want to be asked by my spouse or colleagues why we're not keeping up."

4. Fourth, some churches are driven by a vision to grow, because they know their survival is at stake. They are motivated to pay their bills, so the extent of their vision is in direct proportion to the size of their bills.

Unfortunately, some pastors and churches address this issue by adjusting the break-even point downward. After all, since more than half the expenses of a typical church go toward staff support, then the less money a pastor needs from the church, the smaller size the church can be. Pastoral spouses who work outside the church, second jobs for the pastor, generous relatives, outside donors, and other factors can be used to ensure that the ministerial family poses the most minimal drain possible on the church budget.

If abundant funding does come in, what happens to the vision? For example, suppose a windfall (something you receive as a result of something you do not do) comes your way from the bequest of a well-to-do member who died. This favorable turn of finances does not necessarily remove the limiting survival vision. Instead, it usually demotivates leadership. There is no longer a reason to keep pushing. "We do not have to get out in the fray of battle anymore, so we will take it easy for a while." A church with a sizeable endowment account is almost impossible to motivate to grow.

Or, what if the church does indeed grow and is able to pay its pastoral staff more; will that solve the survival limiter? In other words, will an increased pastoral standard of living affect the motivation for growing a church? Probably not. But, given how most pastors are compensated, I rarely advise them to turn down the pay raise.[2]

5. I call the fifth vision limiter the goal of a generic stand-alone church. In many people's imagination, the ideal church has its own building, presumably painted white with a small steeple, in a comfortable suburb with shade trees over the parking lot. It supports one full-time pastor who can give his wife the opportunity to be a full-time homemaker and can send their children through college. It has no need to enlarge the church facility.

This pastor has a part-time secretary, a part-time custodian, and a part-time organist—not enough staff to create obligations for management, but enough that the nitty-gritty is done by others. Sunday school literature seems written primarily for this idyllic situation.

For many pastors and board members, this vision of a stand-alone church is enough to cause them to reach beyond where they are. Am I criticizing such a church or lifestyle? No. Any light at all that causes you to see a preferred future condition is preferable to no light.

My encouragement is to continue forward, because this vision—like most others—is going to run out at a point that may be short of what God intends.

6. Growth limiter number six involves comfort. This view is conveyed by words like, "If there were only one thousand dollars more in the budget, or just three or four more volunteers, then everything would be just fine."

To detect situations like these, you ask a pastor or church board, "What would you like to see happen here?" If they answer, "Perhaps be 10 percent larger than we are now, so we would be in a more comfortable position," then you can predict that the church will stretch itself for about a year. Such a goal offers an incentive of sorts, but what if God has a greater scope of ministry in mind?

7. Seventh comes the "No Vacancy" sign. Have you driven by a motel and seen a neon light that read, "Sorry, No Vacancy"? Motel managers have a switch inside their office which they activate when the bed level is full enough.

In tight-cash times the switch is not touched until 1:00 A.M. when every room is rented, including the one with the broken TV. In good times, if it is 9:00 P.M. and the proprietors are tired, they flip the switch.

Some churches have a similar system, and they activate the "No Vacancy" indicator at the earliest opportunity possible. If the parking lot is full, or the sanctuary is full, or the Sunday schools are full, do you do anything about it, or just enjoy it? When an opportunity arises for community-wide exposure, such as the hometown sports star coming to your church to give testimony of his faith in Christ, what circumstances lead you to conclude that you have put "enough" energy into publicity?

8. The eighth vision limiter is a fortress mentality in which the wagons are drawn in a circle. I grew up in a very conservative group which taught that we were the only true churches left. If only we had eyes to see from a satellite, we would have realized that the ecclesiastical landscape was filled with scores of denominations of our size and type doing likewise: pulling their wagons together in a very tight circle. Somehow, all of us were the only ones left.

Even so, that climate helped build a fierce sense of morale. Our vision produced strength of camaraderie. It got us out of bed and propelled activity. But it did not necessarily provide the loving context into which others could be accepted.

9. Ninth is what I call home-grown missionaries. I once heard a pastor say, "I have a vision that God will call people from this church to the mission field. It is my intention to stay here and grow this church, so that we have enough giving ability to support every missionary God calls from this church."

My initial impression was, "That sounds like a great goal." His church had commissioned 140 missionaries, and he had built a church of two thousand persons to make good on that pledge.

That was an appropriate vision for him. The problem is that most churches can look back over fifty years of no one entering pastoral ministry or missionary service. Thus, with no one to support, they have no incentive to grow.

10. The tenth vision limiter is the idea of a family staff—a job for all the children as they enter adulthood. If the pastoral couple had nine or ten kids, this vision would give them a high standard to shoot for. But what happens after they have involved all their children plus their spouses? And what about the one- or two-child pastoral family? And in those denominations where the wife is the senior pastor, this vision might backfire!

11. Eleventh is "the restoration of our golden era." Many churches will point to thirty-year-old photographs on the wall that depict the Sunday school covering the whole block. Long-time members will lament, "If we can only rebuild what we had back then."

When I examine the photo I usually see all Anglo faces. Then I go outside and see nothing but African Americans, Hispanics, or Asians. I comment, "We'd have to recolor that photograph for it ever to happen here again." Unfortunately, that often silences them, because their vision of reenacting the past does not allow for an ethnic transition as well.

12. A twelfth limiting vision is closing the back doors. This approach may range from keeping the young people from dropping out to raising the church's visitor-retention ratio.

In some cases, a more blunt description is that of recovering ghosts. The matriarchs and patriarchs of the church can walk through the sanctuary and find people in every empty pew. "That's the Pettits' pew," they will say. If I ask where they are, I am told,

"Oh, they moved to Indiana years ago." Same with the Edwardses who, except for their oldest son, are now in Maryland, and Pam Maas who moved her membership to the church across town six years ago, and the Bartels who were railroaded out of the church by a powerful elder, whose son is head elder today.

These people might come back for a homecoming event or when in town over the holidays, but trying to produce attendance growth from them can be like giving blood to a leukemia victim. If you fail to do something about the bone marrow, you must keep pumping in transfusions.

The idea of building bridges with former members is not wrong. It does reflect a form of vision. It drives some ministry. It may not be all God has in mind, however.

You can invest enormous amounts of energy trying to reach disillusioned or lapsed members, but the old wounds are very hard to heal. As Lyle Schaller and others have pointed out, it is probably two or three times more fruitful to go after unsolicited contacts than to attempt to raise the dead.[3]

13. Thirteenth is the rally or high-visibility event. "Let's sponsor a concert series," someone will say. Or, "Let's have an annual homecoming and get some action going around here." This approach, which rallies the church and boosts the morale, too often produces results that last for only a few weeks. It may momentarily fill the hall, revival style, without regard to whether there is a durable structure underneath. It produces more of an audience than a spiritually connected congregation.

14. The fourteenth vision limiter is a mesa-culture mentality. It says, "We will reach all who can climb to where we are and meet our standards." When these words are translated into denominational terms, it means that the majority of persons in the outside community cannot qualify.

Such groups might vigorously affirm that the gospel is for all people, but at the same time they create subtle entrance requirements, usually of an ethnic nature, that exclude the majority of the surrounding community.

For example, in certain Lutheran churches, the only way to be accepted is to be the child of a German immigrant, or to marry the child of a parishioner, or to have been a foreign exchange student who studied in Germany. Short of that, getting in is very difficult, typically requiring a generation or so. As a result, the outflow is often greater than the inflow.

15. Finally is the outgrown vision. Many a preacher leader has built the largest facility or attendance in town. Such leaders have touched what they knew of need in the community but then lost their vision, because nothing new replaced it. If they fail to seek the Lord for fresh direction, or if through the work of the enemy they become distracted or preoccupied by some intervening mess, they will plateau, rest on their laurels, or even stagnate.

Self-Evaluation Moment

Before reading further, write down a few key words that come to mind to answer each of the following questions:

1. How is your church distinct from most others in your community? What things does your church do particularly well?

2. What will your church's ministry look like five years from now? How will it be different from the present?

3. If money were no object, what would you do differently? If you had an unlimited supply of volunteer energy, what would you do differently?

4. Do your answers to these questions point you to any vision limits? If so, which one(s)?

More Durable Vision

Is there a goal more durable than the fifteen listed above? Will every vision ultimately prove to be inadequate?

Not that anything is inherently wrong with these objectives, limiting as they are. True, sometimes people ask, "What went wrong with our vision?" and the real culprit was a church fight or moral failure. But those distractions can be dealt with, usually on one's knees.

Each factor I have listed is indeed a form of vision. It does inform activity and guide behavior. It focuses people and causes them to cooperate. Each opens the door for a certain growth potential. But, like the governor on a carburetor, it slows you down at a certain point. It may carry you from this week to the next week but will probably not take you to one year, three years, or five years from now.

I propose a dream so enduring that it has yet to be fulfilled. Those who pursue it live with an ongoing resolution in their hearts that they will make a difference in ministry.

This vision-influencing factor, the only one that seems limitless, is to view the thousands of people around you as a harvest field. (I will further describe this limitless harvest in chapter 12.) It comes from Jesus' words to his disciples: "Open your eyes and look at the fields! They are ripe for harvest. Even now the reaper draws his wages, even now he harvests the crop for eternal life. . . . Others have done the hard work, and you have reaped the benefits of their labor" (John 4:35–36, 38). The contrast between this harvest vision and a limited vision is highlighted in Figure 2.

Before you entered the mission field represented by your church, God went first. Before you arrived there, he had already sowed. The prayers of mothers, the gospel preaching of others, and the witness of Christians before you have all been used by God to prepare a harvest.

This means that people are ready to respond to Christ, waiting for whichever representative of Jesus will come to them in a loving, prayerful way. Loving God by loving lost people is the greatest and the only limitless motivator I have ever observed. As Bill Hybels often says in describing his vision for North America's second largest church, Willow Creek Community Church, "Lost people matter to God. Therefore, lost people should matter to me."

> Before you entered the mission field represented
> by your church, God went first.

How to Listen in Prayer

I cannot speak of vision without also underscoring the role of fasting and prayer. In my consulting, when I ask pastors how they seek God on this issue of vision, most will affirm that they make it

Figure 2

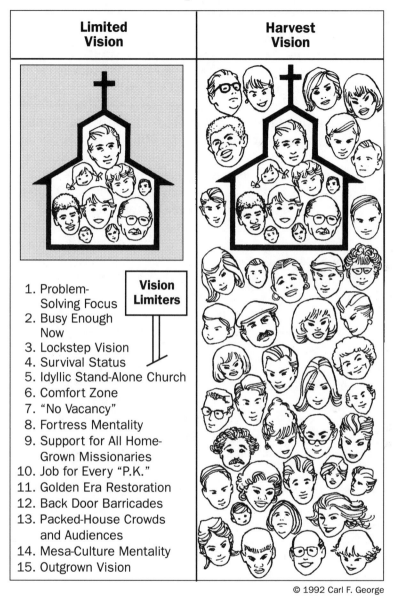

Limited Vision	Harvest Vision

1. Problem-Solving Focus
2. Busy Enough Now
3. Lockstep Vision
4. Survival Status
5. Idyllic Stand-Alone Church
6. Comfort Zone
7. "No Vacancy"
8. Fortress Mentality
9. Support for All Home-Grown Missionaries
10. Job for Every "P.K."
11. Golden Era Restoration
12. Back Door Barricades
13. Packed-House Crowds and Audiences
14. Mesa-Culture Mentality
15. Outgrown Vision

Vision Limiters

their practice to claim such promises as Jesus' words about asking, seeking, and knocking (Matt. 7:7–8).

Almost none of these pastors talk about listening to God. The most common approach, I suspect, is to continue talking while waiting on God to answer. I propose that our fervency in speaking seriously undercuts our ability to hear God's reply.

A story Dr. Cho recounted in my hearing summarizes the essence of what prayer could be all about. He said that when Yoido Full Gospel Church had reached about 300,000 active participants, a pastor from a church of 3,000 came to see him. The pastor said, "Dr. Cho, I need help in understanding something. Like yourself, I'm a Korean and am pastor of a church. But you have 300,000 and I have 3,000, so something does not add up for me."

Then this pastor, without any hint of arrogance, began to compare his background with that of Dr. Cho. "I have an American education, you have studied only at a Bible school here in Korea. In addition, I have examined, as objectively as I can, tape recordings of my sermons and of your sermons. I believe I preach a better sermon. What I don't understand is why, if I preach a better sermon and have a better education, do you have 300,000 people in church and I have 3,000 people."

Dr. Cho said that he answered with a question "Do you pray?"

"Oh, yes," the minister said.

"How much?"

He answered, "I pray daily at least thirty minutes. I've outlined my prayers so that in the course of the week I've prayed for all my obligations here and across the world. I'm very, very conscientious about that."

After pausing, the visiting pastor asked Dr. Cho, "How much do you pray?"

Dr. Cho answered, "Anywhere between one and three hours a day." Then came the clincher. "The difference," Dr. Cho said, "between thirty minutes and one to three hours is the difference between 3,000 and 300,000."

My thoughts raced to my own prayer life. "One to three hours a day?" I asked myself. "What in the world could I say for up to three hours in one day?" After thirty minutes I'm prayed up and am beginning to talk in circles. How does someone pray for hours on end?

Then I realized the Western assumptions through which I was hearing Dr. Cho's story. What kind of a sick neurotic would I have to be to hold a "conversation" in which, nonstop for three hours, I did all the talking?

When we first hear Dr. Cho's story, we think, Okay, take the thirty-minute stuff we do and draw it out five times as much. Try harder and push longer. Greater energy leads to more vigorous praying, according to the Western mind-set.

Does Dr. Cho talk *to* God all that time, or does he talk *with* God? The fundamental redefinition of prayer we need is this: Prayer is not so much an effort as a communion. If I do not give God as much time to talk to me as I spend talking to him, I am off balance. No wonder, then, that I did not receive vision and guidance from him.

> Prayer is not so much an effort
> as a communion.

Prayer Is More than "Trying Harder"

Westerners may believe God honors hard prayer, but that is not always the case in Scripture. For instance, Elijah's style, like that of Avis Car Rentals and of most pastors, seemed to be that of trying harder. In his ordeal with the prophets of Baal, he so exhausted himself that he became suicidally depressed. "Lord," he said (to paraphrase 1 Kings 18 and 19), "I'm done. I'm checking out. Just show me the ring so I can throw in the towel. All I want to do is die."

How did God reply? "Elijah, your prayers are not finished yet. Go down to the cave. Rest. Eat something. Stay down there until you hear from me."

That is when Elijah came up with a smarter idea. After he poured out all his despair to the Lord, he was finally ready to listen. "Elijah," God said, "the work I'm getting ready for you is much bigger than anything done to date. We need another king and a new helper for you."

Elijah went from that place of listening prayer to anoint Elisha the great prophet and to anoint a new king. These people, in turn, did far more than silence four hundred false prophets on Mount Carmel. They cleaned out Baal worship all across Israel.

Self-Evaluation Moment

1. In the last week, how much time per day did you average in prayer?

2. Is your initial reaction, in writing down a specific number, one of guilt for not "doing more"? If so, why do you feel that way?

3. If you were to experiment with listening prayer, how would you do it? For example, where would you go? How much time would you need to block out? What distractions would you anticipate, and how would you deal with them?

4. Will you commit yourself, within the next week, to go before the Lord in listening prayer?

I, too, have experienced the powerful, refreshing results of listening prayer. In seeking God's will about the future of the Charles E. Fuller Institute of Evangelism and Church Growth, where I have served as director since 1978, I once asked God, "How much do I plan for the next ten years? What's this work supposed to look like? What kinds of numbers and sizes should we target? I need your guidance." Not being a charismatic Christian, I have much to learn about hearing a voice from on high. In my prayer times I said, "God, you know I don't hear very well, but I need to know. . . ."

A short time after this session of prayer, I had dinner with a Christian acquaintance who used to attend a Sunday school class with me. Formerly he had been the chief financial officer of a multi-million-dollar corporation. When I asked about his current line of work, he explained that he specialized in helping companies plan for the future. As he talked, I realized that his expertise was in exactly the same areas, though on a bigger scale, as the Institute's needs.

As I continued to listen to God in prayer, I sensed he was saying, "Bring in the brightest, best-trained, most experienced new personnel you can find." So, knowing that we had little more than a dream to offer this man, I asked if he would consider helping us.

To make a long story short, through a series of extraordinary events—including this man's willingness to take a major pay cut—he joined the Charles E. Fuller Institute and has played a significant role in helping us formulate an organizational plan designed to minister to more people in a more effective way than I ever imagined possible.

The Bottom Line in Prayer

What happened? A vision had captured his heart. He began to see that he could make a difference. And no amount of money could substitute for that.

What am I saying? When you learn to pray in such a way that you listen, you will not only find out what God wants to be done, you will begin to learn the by whom, the how, and the when. As a result, you can proceed with enormous boldness. When you are doing God's work in God's way and in God's time, then you are God's person and you are the most invincible force on earth. All the opposition you can face will be irrelevant.

The crucial issue boils down to one of faith: the ability to see what God is ready to do next so that you are in a cooperative attitude as he does that. That is what it means to walk by faith.

When Elijah stood at Mount Carmel, he was not bossing God around. He did not say, "Put the fire there, God," as though this was Elijah's bright idea. The thing that made Elijah a survivor of Mount Carmel was that he knew how far away to stand from that pile of wet wood.

He had heard what God had called him to do and he did not get in the way. His prayer was, "Lord, I am here, because you told me to come here. That wood over there is wet, because you told me to wet it. These people have been gathered together, because you told me to gather them together. So Lord, we are here, simply because we have been following orders."

Until we are aware of God's marching orders, our activities are vain and folly. Bill Hybels wrote a book entitled *Too Busy Not to Pray.* It says, in essence, a human being's "engine" is designed to run at 5,000 RPM, but he was regularly winding his out at 10,000 RPM. He tells of having to slow down, through journaling and other exercises, so that he can hear God.[4]

I have every confidence, then, that the astounding growth of Willow Creek Community Church has come not because Bill Hybels said, "I want the biggest church in North America." No, he said, "I want to abide in Jesus Christ," and then he was able to receive the vision God had for the spiritual harvest the Willow Creek church is to reach.

That is the kind of vision God longs to give to all who will seek him.

For Further Thought

1. Do you agree that each of the fifteen vision limiters described does indeed put a cap on the scope of ministry that a church might try to achieve? Pick six of the vision limiters that seem clearest to you; which biblical principles would support each one?

2. Select four of the vision limiters and give examples for each that would be applicable to your church. Which vision limiter has the strongest influence on your church?

3. In what ways is the following quotation from this chapter applicable to your church? "Before you entered the mission field represented by your church, God went first. Before you arrived there, he had already sowed. The prayers of mothers, the gospel preaching of others, and the witness of Christians before you, have all been used by God to prepare a harvest."

4. How are the experiences of Bill Hybels and Paul Yonggi Cho relevant to the church you now serve? In what way do they challenge you? What has been your experience with "listening prayer"?

5. Summarize in twenty-five words or less your vision for the church you presently serve. In what ways is that vision inadequate when compared with the size of harvest God might use your church to reach?

3

How Does Vision Motivate?

You have a growing conviction of what God is calling your church to be. You see where you are now (point A), what improvements and changes need to be introduced (point B), and where you will move for the future (point C). You are eager, excited.

But now what do you do? You know you cannot start at point C. How do you go to work on point B? And how do you keep from running too fast and getting ahead of yourself?

Communication Counts

Such books as *Leaders: Strategies for Taking Charge,* by Warren Bennis and Burt Nanus, describe how visionary leadership operates. These authors say: "The leader may generate new views of the future and may be a genius at synthesizing and articulating these new views of the future, but this makes a difference only when the vision has been successfully communicated throughout the organization and effectively institutionalized as a guiding principle."[1]

That was the role Fred Smith played for Federal Express. His example (mentioned in the previous chapter) illustrates that the leader's basic philosophy must be: We have seen what this organization can be; here is what the future needs to look like, and how we must act to make it so. A leader is as powerful as the ideas he or she can communicate.

A vision cannot be established in an organization by edict or by the exercise of power or coercion. It is more an act of persuasion, of creating an enthusiastic and dedicated commitment because it is right for the times, right for the organization, and right for the people who are working in it.

Similarly, in Christ's church, God often works through the vision of a leader. Paul Yonggi Cho, founding pastor of the world's largest church, counts more than 55,000 trained cell-group leaders among his 625,000 parishioners. These trained care givers are serving in that role because Dr. Cho had a vision of what would happen if he would release lay people to care for one another. The tools he puts in their hands, the supervision system he has inaugurated, the staff he has hired, all contribute to the vision being a reality.[2]

Did Jesus convey this type of thinking? I believe he spread his vision of the kingdom of God through his analogies and stories. Jesus frequently asked, "What is the kingdom of God like?" His answers were filled with vivid and powerful word pictures: "[It] is like a man who sowed good seed" (Matt. 13:24), or "like a mustard seed" (13:31) or "like yeast" (13:33). When a pastor today says, "What is the church like?" or "I have a dream," and then uses an analogy to describe a preferred future, that minister is likewise casting or communicating the vision.

Sermon lore contains the story of an elocutionist who visited a church and read aloud Psalm 23. Then an old man, who was a long-time member and had suffered greatly over the years, stood up and prayed. In his conversation with God he quoted that same Psalm.

The audience did not applaud him as they did the public speaker. Instead, they wept. Afterward someone said to the elocutionist, "Can you account for the difference in how these people responded to you and how they responded to him?" He replied, "Yes, I knew the Psalm and he knew the shepherd." The veteran follower of Christ knew more than the written Word of God. He had communed

> When a vision comes from the altar of God,
> it transforms people who are in the presence of that vision.

with the Creator of the universe and had been shaped by the vision of his best Friend.

How Is Vision Cast (Communicated)?

Three elements, when combined, help people believe a vision and take ownership in it.

1. First, you need a game plan. What is your outline for making the most effective use of your pastoral leaders' abilities for the lives of your staff and your lay people? What is your strategy to best enable lay people to give greatest support to their pastor's plans for the church?

For some churches the formula is as simple as this: Celebrate in festivals and care in cells. Another way to describe that particular game plan would be to say the goal is to multiply the ministry of Jesus by empowering lay leaders to provide pastoral care to groups of about ten people.

The game plan, then, is your philosophy of ministry. It summarizes your overall strategy and objectives. It needs to be clear enough that you could present it in three or four sentences to your unchurched neighbor who asks, "Exactly what is your church trying to do?"

Here are some game plans that convey a focused direction for a church:

"Our purpose is loving God, caring for one another, and reaching the world for Christ."

"God is building an ever-stronger church, with ongoing emphasis on evangelism, discipleship, and nurture, that will reach metro (name of city) and beyond."

"Our vision is to touch our world with the love of Christ as we grow in his Spirit and reach out in love, motivated by a passion for Christ and compassion for others."

"Using every available opportunity in all walks of life to lovingly persuade the world to become committed followers of Jesus Christ and responsible members of his growing kingdom, that they may do the same."

"Our mission is to be a worshiping people, a caring community, a preaching center, an equipping network, and a worldwide witness."

2. A second factor that helps the vision is the party line. In other words, how are the various truths of the faith handled at your church? Which are perceived as having high priority? Examples of party line are: "We don't do tongues here"; "If you want the church to pray for healing, ask the elders to come and anoint you with oil"; and "Unless you lead a home-cell group, you cannot get elected to office at this church." The party line, then, may deal with some very ticklish issues. But it is a necessary ingredient in explaining how a vision will be communicated.

3. A third component of effective vision casting is hero making. Michael LeBoeuf in his book *The Greatest Management Principle in the World*[3] says, in essence, "What gets rewarded gets done." The implication for pastors and church leaders is to keep score and then brag on the things they want to see more of.

Christians profit from positive role models, whether they come from the hall of champions in Hebrews chapter 11, from Sunday-school-teacher-of-the-month profiles in church bulletins, or from hero-making sermons. As the old adage goes, "Everybody loves a story." One of the reasons for the renewed interest in narrative preaching is that people love to learn about people. Stories communicate vision as they set a norm for what it means to be a winner.

Self-Evaluation Moment

Which of the following persuasion methods would best represent your style of vision casting? Which example includes all above-mentioned elements of vision casting?

1. I want to thank everyone who contributed to the Christmas food drive and to announce that, probably due to everybody being so busy, only Nathan Kenion had the time to deliver the baskets. You need to thank him, and to make a little extra time next year when we run the food drive. It's important, you know!

2. Did everyone hear how Nathan Kenion made sure every food basket was delivered on Christmas Eve? That's the kind of ministry our church wants to be known for! Thanks to Nathan's initiative, we showed twenty new households what it means to know Christ and make him known.

3. I'm happy to report that our food drive was a great success, and that we made sure every basket was delivered by Christmas Eve. We on the staff really feel supported by you, and we're glad that we got this very special project accomplished.

Only example 2 incorporates all three elements of vision casting in positive terms. Example 1 affirms that the food drive is "very important" to the game plan, appeals to guilt and duty as the party line, and makes a hero of Nathan. Example 3 speaks of the food drive as a special project, urges loyalty to the staff as the party line, and makes heroes of the staff, not of Nathan.

What Helps Prevent Vision Failure?

To be better prepared to launch your vision in your church, you need to consider four ingredients that need to be in place before you can safely assume that the vision is complete. Our field observations of actual leaders and churches confirm that prematurity is the most common cause of vision failure.

1. First, know that the vision answers the *what* question. In other words, you see what God wants accomplished in this particular place.

The mature vision maker will take the *what* information and start running. But knowing what to do is only part of the guidance God intends to give.

2. Second, know *how* God wants it done. Numerous Old Testament accounts illustrate that God not only told his children what he wanted them to do, but he frequently told them how to do it. The procedures for constructing the ark, the tabernacle, and many other elements of God's plan were spelled out in enormous detail. The *how* was very significant.

3. Third, know *by whom* the vision should be done. God almighty, creator and overseer of the entire universe, frequently thought it important to spell out who should be involved in the process. "Use the tribe of Judah to start the battle against the Benjamites' left-handed slingers" (see Judg. 20:13–18), or "I have filled Bezalel with the Spirit of God and with skill, ability, and knowledge" in the crafts needed for the tabernacle construction (see Exod. 31:1–11; 35:30–36:1).

God often fingers the specific talents he wants to use.

This specific guidance was evidenced recently in Loren Cunningham's work with Youth With A Mission. He tells of speaking to a crowd of several hundred and noticing, in particular, a young man wearing a green sweater. After the meeting, Cunningham's wife, Darlene, told her husband that not only did the same eighteen-year-old catch her attention, but that she heard God tell her to "speak to a boy in a green sweater" about coming on their summer program.

Darlene found the young man and related to him what God had told her minutes before. The youth was dumbfounded. He kept hitting his chest with his open palm. "Uh, I . . . I just asked God to have one of you speak to me personally if he wanted me to go!"

The book containing this account, *Is That Really You, God?*[4] observes that in the twenty years between the "green-sweater" event and the writing of the book, an enormously fruitful ministry came out of that person. God gave Loren and Darlene Cunningham "by whom" guidance. God answers the "by whom" question in numerous ways: Scripture illuminated by the Holy Spirit, godly counsel, impressions on the heart, divinely shaped circumstances, and—as with the Cunninghams—the still, small voice of God. The key is to be aware that "by whom" issues are of great significance. They play an important role in how a vision takes shape.

4. Know *when* is the right time to act. I once sat with Christian philosopher Francis Schaeffer. I said, "Dr. Schaeffer, the genius of your ministry draws on your ability to stroke your beard in a hesitating way, and then to offer very simple maxims, timed in such a way and with such an inimitable style that people are leaning forward in eagerness to hear what you will say next. That dynamic is perfect for video and film. You would bestow a wonderful gift on evangelical Christianity if you would allow yourself to be filmed

walking along some outdoor trail in Switzerland and commenting on life."

He stroked his beard (of course!) and said, "Hmmm. This is confirming."

After pausing (of course!) he said, "It will take a great deal of discernment and prayer for me to know who the production company should be, what the visual format should look like, and whether it is God's time yet or not."

Two years later, the film series *How Shall We Then Live?* was released. It produced such a widespread impact, I believe, because Dr. Schaeffer had not grabbed a general idea and started running with it. Rather, the vision had matured. He understood all the pieces before he moved.

Scripture abounds with illustrations of how God sometimes moves very quickly. Those examples do not mean that God is in a hurry, however. The king's business requires haste, but God is not hasty.

> The king's business requires haste,
> but God is not hasty.

What Vision Can Do

In one twelve-month period, the worship attendance at Willow Creek Community Church near Chicago jumped by almost 3,000. It grew from an average weekly attendance of 5,606 in 1985 to one high-attendance Sunday of 8,248 in 1986.

At that time, I asked Bill Hybels, the founding pastor, "What does it feel like to experience a 50 percent jump in one year's time?"

He said, "We had no idea how rapidly the growth would occur; it caught us completely by surprise. We fill the auditorium twice, and have to bring in folding chairs as well."

Then he made a comment that revealed the scope of his vision. "We're really struggling," he said, "because no one is willing to bar our doors and say to lost people who drive into our parking lot, 'We haven't made provision for you to hear the gospel today. You'll have to go home now.'"

I asked Pastor Hybels what he was planning to do. He shook his head. "We don't know fully. We've prayed, we've sought, we've searched. We think we're going to try a Saturday-night service. We're not sure it will work, but we've got to do something."

I said, "Have you ever wanted to quit growing?"

He answered, "There was a time when I remember us saying, 'Hey, we've grown enough. Let's cool it for a while.'"

He continued, "We decided to change our focus. Instead of trying to make every Sunday more appealing than the week before, I'd launch a ten-week series on the Ten Commandments. That was the most unexciting topic for unsaved people I could think of. I figured it would cap the growth and give us a breather.

"To our surprise, our attendance increased by one thousand during that series! We felt like God reached down and slapped us. Soundly rebuked, I said, 'Lord, we won't ever try to slow you down again!'"

Bill Hybels, who believes his primary spiritual gift is leadership, understands the what, how, by whom, and when components of vision. By the grace of God, his maturity of vision will result in the church continuing to go forward.

(It turns out that Willow Creek's Saturday night service, implemented in 1989, was so well received that they later added a second Saturday-night service and a second midweek service as well.)

Needed: A Balanced Team

I am often asked, "Can *any* godly leader improve his or her vision-implementing skills? Can I develop ways of thinking that will give me a more consistent performance and higher-quality decisions than at present?" I believe the answer is yes.

Surveys show that most pastors and lay leaders excel either as doers or as dreamers, but not as both. That is, some preoccupy themselves with activity and implementation, while others spend lots of time thinking of great things to be done for God but do not know how to transform those dreams into reality. For greatest effectiveness, a leader must know how to provide direction by both dreaming and doing.[5]

Many pastors and key lay people have not reached their full,

God-given potential in how to lead a team that can make things happen. Certain techniques, skills, and sensitivities can help them move from being do-aholics or idealists to being actual leaders.

Joel Barker, a best-selling author on the topic of paradigm shifts, says, "A leader is someone you will follow to a place you wouldn't go by yourself."[6] In other words, a leader is someone who has a follower. No functional definition of leadership will hold up in the absence of followers.

To increase one's effectiveness at influencing a "followership," a leader needs to maintain balance on both the "dreaming" and the "doing" portions of providing direction.

But there is more to leadership. According to Max DePree, former board chairman of an evangelical seminary and chief executive officer of a multimillion-dollar business, "In the art of leadership . . . the first responsibility of a leader is to define reality."[7] Leaders cause their followers to know what is important and what is not. Whether in church or business, they describe the landscape, articulate the plan of action, and rally the troops to join in the effort.

How, then, does a leader or leadership team begin to implement God's vision for a particular church?

1. The first step is to clearly articulate the desired outcome. In other words, what do you believe God wants to see happen? Obviously, if you do not know what the improvement is supposed to look like, then you will not know when you have arrived.

In Bill Hybels's case, the desired outcome was that Willow Creek would never have to turn anyone away who comes seeking God. For him and his leadership team, this vision means keeping enough open seats in the auditorium so as not to create a turn-away factor.

2. The second step in implementing vision is to tackle the blockage problem. What is preventing the outcome from taking place? That question requires some analysis. Sometimes the answer is obvious. Other times the formula is so complicated that you need help, such as from a professional consultant, to identify the blockage.

For example, several years ago, a pastor said to me, "I've been studying our church and I think we're experiencing sociological strangulation."

I asked for his evidence.

"Well," he said, "our attendance has plateaued at 120 and we need a larger auditorium." It turned out, however, that his present auditorium held 200 seats. Strangulation does not occur until a church exceeds 80 percent—160 seats, in this case.[8]

"I don't think tearing down your auditorium and building it larger is really the answer," I said. "Let's talk about your Christian education space. If you started a new Sunday school class tomorrow, where would you place it?"

"In one of the empty rooms down at the end of the hall," he quickly responded. "We're temporarily using them for storage."

"Well," I said, "the Sunday school doesn't seem to be in trouble. So we haven't identified the blockage yet. How about parking?"

"We're in great shape," he answered. "We just paved the alley behind the church and we gained twelve parking spaces."

My surveys have shown that the average car on a Sunday morning contains about 2.3 people. (That's a husband with a wife who is three months pregnant!) So, with an attendance of 120, he would need just over fifty parking spaces.

"What does the rest of your parking look like?" I asked.

"Those twelve new spaces represent our entire on-premises parking," he said.

"Oh! Where do the other forty or so cars park?" I queried.

"They park curbside," he said.

"What distance do they have to walk from curbside?"

"Oh, one or two hills."

I suspected we had found the blockage. "Hills? Do you have much ice here during the winter?"

"Sure, lots, but our people get used to it."

"Do you plow the sidewalks?"

"What sidewalks?"

Now I knew we had found a major problem. "What about a woman with heels and carrying a baby?"

"It's an adventure, but our people can handle it!" he acknowledged with a smile.

"Where do you park *your* car?" I asked. I could not understand how this intelligent pastor had missed the significance of the parking issue.

"In my garage," he explained. "It's in the manse next door to the church. One or two other families also live adjacent to the church building, and all we do is walk across the alley."

Here was a pastor who could not see his problem with low parking capacity, because he never had to use the lot. Nor did two other families, who happened to be opinion leaders on the church board.

3. The third step in vision implementation is to act. I suggested to the pastor that the church tear down the manse and make the property into a parking lot. However, in his denomination that was unthinkable, especially since the manse looked like a historical artifact from the frontier era.

Even if my proposal were unacceptable, and the Lord did not send a lightning bolt, the church at least knew what issue to work on. Eventually, as I recall, it bought a nearby empty lot and made it suitable for parking.

This process of moving from outcome statement to blockage identification to action is not intuitive. Most church leaders are talented for one of these steps but not all three.

People who are drawn to outcome issues tend to be visionaries, while people who live near the action box tend to be doers. What about those skilled in detecting blockages? I call them observers or analysts. Such people are rarely pastors.

Depending on how God has wired you, one of these categories will seem most natural for you. Chances are that you seldom venture willingly beyond the comfort of that arena.[9]

Self-Evaluation Moment

It's fun to guess the motivation of different people in your church. (Or, would only an analyzer make a statement like that?) With which of the following people do you most closely identify? Which is most like your spouse, your pastor, or another member of the pastoral team?

Maria: She sits at meetings strumming her fingers or tapping her foot. She loves to make lists, with lots of specifics, down to the exact quantities of postage and coffee needed. "Now that's real planning," she'll say. When the pastor or chair talks about the grand purposes and ideals envisioned for the church, she says, "Let's get on with it! When are we going to

do something?" (Maria's drawback: If she alone were directing the planning process, she'd churn out lists of things to do,
but they may go nowhere, because her action steps would not
necessarily address the blockages that lead to an outcome.)
Maria is a doer.

Charlie: He begins many comments with "I noticed that . . ."
or "I was thinking about. . . ." At the same time, he does not
seem motivated to solve the problem; he would much rather
talk about it—or find another conundrum to untangle. (Charlie's drawback: If he alone were directing the planning
process, he would inspire great discussions and marvelous
insight, but little action.) Charlie is an observer.

Pete: He doesn't even like planning meetings. He's forever
talking about the purposes of God and what God wants to see
done at the church. He becomes so passionate about his
dreams for the ministry that people rib him about not being
able to eat breakfast in the morning until he's had at least
twelve new ideas. (Pete's drawback: If he alone were directing the planning process, he might become very frustrated
that the church is more on dead center than exploding with
vitality. In addition, he probably wouldn't be able to figure
out why the process is not working.) Pete is a visionary.

Making It Work

A Methodist pastor in Philadelphia, known as the most advanced
urban-ministries person in his section of the district, once said to
me, "Now I finally understand why I've been spinning my wheels
for the last five years."

I asked him to explain. He told me about an earlier era at the
same church, which was quite successful. "I'm an idea man," he
said. "I'd get an inspiration, and then it would turn into ministry."

As we talked, it became clear that he was a visionary. He did not
know *how* his ideas had translated into ministry, because a layman
in his church had taken care of that.

"This guy spent his entire life organizing labor unions," the minister explained. "When he retired, he got converted, joined our

church, and hung around my elbow. I'd give someone a wonderful ministry idea and, as I turned to talk with somebody else, he'd go off to the side with whomever I'd just talked to and suggest ways to implement my suggestions. Before I knew it, they had a whole ministry planned.

"He'd come back, listen to me talking to the next person, follow that person, and give that individual some guidelines as well.

"Ever since this man died," continued the minister, "I haven't made a lick of progress."

His summary statement was telling. "Until just now I didn't realize what that guy did for our church. I visualized, and he organized."

This Methodist minister had found someone whose forte was the observer's box, who analyzed, helped the doers get their task lists together, and translated vision into an "actionable" game plan.

In whichever area you excel, do you see what you can do? If you are going to move beyond yourself, link up with people whose strengths differ from yours. Doing so could give birth to a complete problem-solving team.[10]

For Further Thought

1. Recall from Scripture some of Jesus' commands that communicate a strong sense of vision. What are some experiences in the Book of Acts in which the church struggled with the issue of vision? What specific vision did God give the apostle Paul for his ministry? Peter?

2. Think of a recent goal that your church met with great success. Review how well the what, how, by whom, and when components were articulated. What correlation do you see between successful implementation and maturity of vision? What would be an example of a premature vision in your fellowship?

3. Among your pastoral leadership and church board, who are the visionaries? the analyzers? the doers? If you have had a recent change of pastoral leadership, what were the strengths of the previous minister? What expectations were then transferred to the successor?

4. Think about the last time you tried to "sell" a new idea to someone in your church. Did you include elements of the game plan? of party line? of hero making?

4

How Would a Church-Growth Consultant Describe Your Church?

It is common knowledge that people with diabetes can live healthy, productive lives if they can receive regular injections of insulin.

When the human body breaks down food, sugars enter the blood, the pancreas produces insulin to regulate the blood's glucose level. If that fails, the result is diabetes, a condition that causes dangerous health effects: weight loss, increasing weakness and melancholy, failure of vital organs, and finally coma and death.

Because scientific researchers have discovered the essential role that the pancreas's production of insulin plays in human health, they developed a way to inject quantities of it into the bloodstream of a diabetic person, so that the metabolizing of sugars occurs as if the pancreas were functioning normally.

Systems Thinking as a Helpful Tool

What these researchers have done is called **systems thinking**. They asked, What does the body do with sugar? What hormone is necessary to regulate carbohydrate metabolism, to control the blood sugar? As they trace the effects of sugar through the human system and find what is not functioning well, they can compensate for it.

Systems thinking, then, leads to accurate diagnosis and intelligent compensation.

> Systems thinking, then, leads to accurate diagnosis
> and intelligent compensation.

Systems thinking, likewise, is needed in a church each time someone asks questions such as, Why are we growing, or not growing? Where are leaders being developed, or not developed? What needs to be fixed? If the pancreas is not operative, do we need a substitute for it?

An important step, then, in analyzing whatever growth barrier your church faces is to examine what has worked in the past and what has not. In short: Why, humanly speaking, has your church grown, or not grown?

Self-Evaluation Moment

Before reading further, apply a systems perspective to your church.

1. What are the top two factors God has used to produce growth in your church over the years?

2. What, at present, is not functioning well?

3. How does that insulin equivalent need to be replaced or compensated for?

Bayer, Bufferin, or Generic?

Let me carry the idea of a systems perspective one step further by using the analogy of aspirin research.

I liken the state of the church today to the pharmaceutical industry of the late nineteenth century. Back then, German laboratories were learning to identify and synthesize compounds. One of their developments is what we today call aspirin.

The substance, consumed by the American public at the rate of twenty tons a year, is a derivative of an acid found in the bark of a willow tree. For centuries people had found relief from their toothaches, headaches, joint pains, and the like by chewing on willow bark. In time, various manufacturers sold extracts of willow bark.

As the study of pharmacology developed, researchers analyzed the family of willow trees to find the active ingredients that relieved people's pain. Was the yellow color necessary? No, that came from the tar on the bark. How about the crunchiness? No, that was the fiber that gives the bark its firmness. What about the bitter taste? Yes, that stems from the compound itself.

In 1893 Felix Hoffman, of the Bayer Company of Germany, developed a commercial process for the production of acetylsalicylic acid. He and his colleagues could do so because they had come to understand the molecular structure, and thus the active ingredients, of what was to become the world's most widely used medication.

The net result is that when you swallow or chew an aspirin tablet, you can be confident that all the vital ingredients have been included. You know that your Bayer, Bufferin, Anacin, or generic-brand aspirin will contribute to your getting better.

The same story could be told of the sociology of church organizations. All our various denominations have been chewing willow bark or willow extract. As we study the different things that work, however, we begin to distinguish between the necessary active ingredients and the nice-to-have peripheral stuff like orange color or cherry flavor.

Similarly, by clearly identifying the underlying compounds at work in churches, we can relieve a lot more pain without the distractions of tree tar, sap, dust, bugs, and everything else that may accompany our bark.

Conversely, if we try to build a church on methodology alone, we will wind up chewing on a panacea that offers no long-term relief to our pain, fever, and inflammation.

> If we try to build a church on methodology alone, we will wind up chewing on a panacea that offers no long-term relief to our pain, fever, and inflammation.

Not What You May Think

Many pastors and lay leaders, in answering the question of why their church has grown or not grown, experience an eye-opening revelation. My discoveries on this topic trace back some twenty years.

After being reared in Miami and educated elsewhere in the South, I became a pastor in Gainesville, Florida. As a result, I thought I was a southerner. At the Gainesville church, however, one of our visitors, a big, pompous surgeon, walked in, stamped his foot, and said, "This is a northern church. I like it, and I'll be back."

My first thought was, "How could he sum us up like that? What makes us northern? How could he so misdiagnose us?"

I thought I already knew the difference between the two. In many southern churches they compliment the preacher for his histrionics, his sweat, and the fact that he uses guilt motivation to trample on people's toes. I thought I qualified.

Then a highway patrolman visited the church. When I returned the call, he said, "Your church is as real as my thumb, preacher, but I won't be back."

"Why not?" I asked.

"Because you're not a southern church," he said.

I was hearing two witnesses, one intellectually arrogant and another a common country fellow, and they both said the same thing.

Some years later, a teacher who became my mentor, C. Peter Wagner, helped me make sense of what had transpired. My dad was from Gallipolis, Ohio, and my mother was from Kearney, Nebraska. Those midwestern German and English backgrounds influenced me more than all the palm trees of Miami. The genetics and culture I carried, even the way I perceived humor, was something as midwestern as if I were a pastor in Peoria, Illinois.

With guidance from Dr. Wagner and others, I reflected on that pastorate and discovered the people drawn to our church were largely from Iowa, Michigan, Illinois, Ohio, Pennsylvania, and New York.

Why did these northerners come under my leadership? I used to think it was my God-given charisma. As it turns out, I had not captivated them; I was merely the least bad of their options.

When they came to our town they scouted around for a Baptist church. Gainesville boasted twelve Baptist churches of the southern variety, but only our church represented the northern variety. No one had noticed that the reason our church was growing was because midwesterners were migrating to our area.

I thought I was there by the call of God, and I was. But he knew more about cultural match than I did, and that is probably why I was brought to that place. I think the Lord looked at what he had going down there and said, "I'm missing a midwestern unit in that region. If I bring that fellow named George over to Gainesville, it will all work." The church was a wonderful success, but because of factors that were beyond my awareness.

If you had asked me why the church went from zero to 650 in nine years, I, like most pastors, would have offered a ready reply: "We preach the Bible." At that point in my own development, I was not trained in social research, so it never occurred to me to test that proposition. What if I had investigated all the other churches in that region to find out how many others were teaching the Bible as God's authoritative word? Had I done so, I would have discovered many churches with that same conviction, yet little growth to show for it.

Genuine Conversion Growth?

I also made another humbling discovery. I had thought God was using my preaching to lead most of our newcomers to faith in Christ.

It turns out that six of ten people who came into our church had already converted somewhere else. And of the four who "walked the aisle" (the tradition in our church), most had already made their decision to accept Christ before they came to that service.

The picture became more clear when I began consulting. I remember walking into an old Lutheran church and being introduced as Pastor George. My speech does not betray an accent, and, based on a name like George, I do not seem to have German roots, as many Lutherans do.

I sensed that the people were having trouble accepting me. Then, when I mentioned that my wife is an Erhard, their suspicions noticeably lessened.

"Oh, an Erhard, how nice," they responded. "This is the man who married the German girl." I was in! My reception had nothing to do with my intellectual credentials, my doctrine, or my ability as a leader. The critical event occurred when I married into the "right" family.

I saw this happen in other communions as well, like the time I met a fellow named Jones who was ministering in the Covenant Church. I said, "That's strange. I've never met a Jones who rose to national prominence in a Swedish denomination." He said, "If you knew my wife's maiden name, you'd understand."

What is this? The gospel is for "whosoever will," but you cannot cut it in many circles if you fail to marry the right person, if your name is not pronounced a certain way, or if your ancestors do not go back to the "right" country.

Why? Humans are complex beings with accompanying roots, preferences, heritage, and language, all of which convey their values. Like it or not, each human is a culture-carrying being. We each have a spirit, of course. But the more significant factor in our ability to attract and recruit people to a church often has to do with the fact that our roots give us an inside track to those people with similar roots.

This view sounds somewhat deterministic. But the determinism apparently exists whether I am aware of it or not. I must accept a powerful reality. People do not like me because of my sweetness, but they respond to my words because of certain commonalties of culture. My background enables me to communicate with their dreams and hopes, and to hold out to them a vision of a better future in which God is redemptive and Jesus is real.

Why Your Church Has Grown

Donald McGavran, founder of America's church growth movement, tells of interviewing one pastor of a growing church who gave the following as the principal reason for its growth: "We preach the Bible as the Word of God and are faithful to it." Then McGavran asked the pastor of the church across the street why he thought his church had *not* grown for the last ten years. His answer, word-for-word, was the same: "We preach the Bible as the Word of God and are faithful to it."[1]

Peter Wagner agrees: "It may not be obvious at first, but it is a fact that many pastors of growing churches have only vague insights into the reasons why their churches are growing."[2] My book *Prepare Your Church for the Future* identifies sixteen different growth sources that most church leaders have either observed or experienced. Here is a summary of those growth sources, which in themselves may be effective methodologies (see also Figure 3):

Preaching and Revivals

Your church revolves around enthusiastic, firebrand preaching or has experienced genuine revival from an outpouring of the Holy Spirit.

Sunday School

Your church's growth is fueled by Sunday school momentum.

Bus Ministry

Your church reaches new families through bus captains who knock on doors and shuttle children to special programming.

Feeder and Receptor Patterns

Your church recycles Christians from other churches.

Intentional Positioning

Your church targets a specific population segment.

Music Center

Your church attracts musicians and other art lovers through a continual cycle of performances, choirs, and ensembles.

Pulpit Teaching and Oratory Skills

Your church is known as a teaching center where people's notebooks may be bigger than their Bibles.

Miracle Ministry

Your church focuses on such signs and wonders as healing and deliverance.

Capture-by-Committee Involvement

Your church builds loyalty by putting newcomers on a committee as soon as possible.

Day Schools

Your church sponsors a Christian school, which serves as a bridge for people to participate in other church activities.

Next-Door-to-the-Right-Institution Syndrome

Your church draws from a nearby denominational college, hospital, or other institution.

High-Visibility and High-Profile Guests

Your church features a steady stream of media personalities.

Appealing, Mixed-Media Seeker Services

Your church combines preaching, artistic ensembles, and multimedia entertainment targeted at the unchurched.

Multiple Staff

Your church staff is comprised of gifted evangelists who pour the bulk of their energies into visitation and outreach.

Immigration and Colonization

Your church is a large ethnic community, such as Scandinavians or Cambodians.

Subcongregations of Adults

Your church is a collection of large Sunday schools, women's ministries, or other sizable groups.[3]

What an abundance of variables that can combine into a growth pattern! Little wonder that we church leaders have such a hard time making sure our "pancreas" is working—or injecting something to fill in for the insulin that the pancreas fails to produce.

Pacesetters for Every Decade

Pastors and lay leaders continually scan the continent for methodologies they find to be impressive and encouraging. In every decade, a different set of high-visibility growing churches have influenced North America's perception or the "insulin injection" needed for greatest church health.

In the 1940s, people trekked to Dallas, Texas, to observe the ministry of W. A. Criswell at First Baptist Church. Or they went to Chattanooga, Tennessee, to see Lee Roberson's great fellowship, Highland Park Baptist Church, with its thirty or more preaching centers.

If you came along a decade later you would have found a different set of churches occupying that special niche of most imitated. Bus-ministry Sunday school centers were coming of age, so in both the 1950s and 1960s you would have traveled to one of several places that had burst into superchurch and megachurch size, such as Jack Hyles's First Baptist Church of Hammond, Indiana, Dallas

Figure 3
16 Growth Methods

1. Preaching and Revivals

2. Sunday School

3. Bus Ministry

4. Feeder and Receptor Patterns

5. Intentional Positioning

6. Music Center

7. Pulpit and Oratory

8. Miracle Ministry

9. Capture by Committee

10. Day Schools

11. Next-Door-to Right-Institution

12. High-Visibility Guests

13. Mixed-Media Seeker Services

14. Multiple Staff

15. Immigration and Colonization

16. Subcongregations of Adults

© 1992 Carl F. George

Billington's Akron Baptist Temple in Ohio, or Jerry Falwell's Thomas Road Baptist Church in Lynchburg, Virginia.

By the mid 1960s, new influence centers included the folk mass, the Jesus-people churches, the new charismatic phenomenon, and the larger-than-life intimacy of the body-life movement. As but one example, the church we know today as Calvary Chapel, of Santa Ana, California, pastored by Chuck Smith, built such astonishing youth and music programs that anyone who could make the journey came to listen and learn.

In the 1970s, the new pacesetters were the major churches forced out of denominations, such as Central Church, Memphis, Tennessee, or First Baptist Church, Modesto, California.

During the 1980s, the rising stars tended to be the media centers. The Crystal Cathedral, led by Robert Schuller, rose to prominence in the late 1970s and through its television broadcast gained widespread attention during the 1980s. In one year a quarter of a million people visited to understand its approach to reaching the unchurched.

The present decade has given rise to a new series of highly influential churches. Willow Creek Community Church, based in greater Chicago and led by founding pastor Bill Hybels, has broken new ground in its use of seeker-sensitive services, team ministry, and drama and other multimedia.

Willow Creek has wielded an amazingly wide influence, because it has been emulated not only by thousands of noncharismatic independent churches, but even mainliners such as Lutherans have adopted "presentational evangelism," as they tend to call the Willow Creek model.

Mistaking the Clothing for the Life Underneath

From Jack Hyles to Bill Hybels, from Chuck Smith to Jerry Falwell, each of these stellar churches, in introducing its ministry, tries to articulate why it does what it does. In general, the more plausible and persuasive its explanations, the larger a magnet it becomes, and the more publicity it receives.

Two potential pitfalls accompany this process, however. First, pilgrims to these various thriving churches sometimes take the attitude back home, even if unintentionally, that "if you haven't visited such-and-such a church and aren't using their approach, you're out of it."

If you go to Second Baptist of Houston, for example, you will undoubtedly be inspired with its passion to reach the lost, even if the manifestation of that zeal is for the staff, stripped to the waist, to enter a wrestling ring for one of their excitement-building contests. This is a high-energy, aggressive, vibrant church.

The church also talks about constructing the largest church facility in Texas. Its campus, with a financial value approaching $100 million, covers acres of buildings. It is both elegant and massive; it fits the "oil sheik" aura of Houston.

While that architectural approach may work in Texas, it is probably inappropriate for Manhattan or downtown Los Angeles. And while entertainment evangelism and attendance contests clearly succeed in many communities, they are not necessarily a copyable philosophy of ministry for a church, say, trying to reach the academic community in an Ivy League university.

Second, and more importantly, when pastors and lay leaders visit these influence centers, they inevitably go home willing to be innovative and motivated to make changes. But they sometimes try to change their church's clothing rather than the living organism underneath. They have gone to a conference and perceived a method rather than the underlying vital ingredients.

Why does this happen? Maybe the high-visibility church misarticulates why it is growing. Maybe the observer misunderstands the presentation. Or maybe both.

The paradigms in this book are by and large transparent to specific methodologies or worship styles. I believe churches grow best if they find a model that God is blessing. Apparently, then, God is working through a number of different models, from traditional to contemporary, and the many nuances in between.

Churches grow best
if they find a model God is blessing.

But there is more to growth than ministry methodology. The more important issue, no matter what the outward approach looks like, is the multiplication of ministry through groups and teams.

Does a church, and especially its pastor, embody a strong vision for an enlarged harvest? Is a strong desire for growth present? Does the leadership know how to best allocate its time and energy through leadership development and groups? These kinds of issues are the real keys to a more vital future.

The Rationale Behind This Chapter

If a team of church growth consultants tried to describe your church, what themes would they highlight? No doubt they would examine growth sources and methodologies being used.

But they would also look underneath and ask if a systemic understanding were informing your perspective. They would probe to make sure you understood how the "insulin" of ministry was being supplied. They would want to make sure that you have distinguished between the cherry flavoring of your aspirin and the molecular compound underneath. In so doing they would point to such issues as vision and ranching.

The purpose of this chapter is to introduce you to systems thinking so that you can make a more accurate diagnosis of your church and therefore more intelligently build on what is essential and compensate for what may be missing.

My point is not to identify a methodology and then leave you there. It is, rather, to help you understand that growth involves more than methodologies, to warn you that many churches misinterpret their growth sources, and to affirm that the most important issue is the vital ingredients of the aspirin, not the color, size, or brand of the particular aspirin tablet.

Armed with this perspective, you are more ready than ever to break barriers to growth.

For Further Thought

1. Look over the list of sixteen growth methodologies in this chapter. Which three have most contributed to the growth of your church?

2. What are some of the misconceptions circulating around your church as to why it has grown or not grown?

3. Based on the "vital ingredients" analogy of aspirin research, what, do you think, are the core factors for the spiritual health and ministry enlargement of any church? Select your top three choices and explain why they are important or will work.

4. What are some of the high-visibility churches that have most influenced you? How would you distinguish between their methodology and their underlying active ingredients?

5. Is there a biblical basis for the idea of one church influencing or mentoring another, or for the concept of more "senior" pastors mentoring newcomer pastors? If yes, could that training encompass spiritual formation? managerial skills? organizational insights?

5

Do You Have
a Growth Bias?

A recent book on spiritual abuse quotes a parish newsletter in which a pastor urged his people to attend church more regularly:

Let me give you an inside look at what goes through your pastor's mind when he notices you aren't coming to all the services provided by the church.

1.   He must be really sick. (He'll be back when he's better.)
2.   Perhaps he got called in to work. (He'd be here if he could.)
3.   Maybe he's out of town. (Just a temporary absence.)
4.   He's upset with me about something. (Uh-oh!)
5.   He thinks I'm a terrible preacher. (How many others think that, too?)
6.   He's looking for a different church to attend. (Gulp!)
7.   He's in his backyard burning his hymnal and Sunday school lesson outlines. (I'm a total failure as a pastor.)[1]

What is the reason people come to church? To find God? To find life? To worship? None of these, according to this newsletter clipping: The primary reason is to make sure the pastor does not feel like a total failure.

Many pastors and lay leaders gain their value at church from how they perform. Their sense of security, and their evaluation of their church's overall spiritual health, is heavily influenced by whether they are well liked, needed, appreciated, and affirmed.

Leaders and Performers

My prayer in writing this book is that the Spirit of God will grant readers new insight into the nature of ministry. That perspective will lead you from being a provider of care *to* your people to being an arranger of care *for* your people. In the process, the spotlight of ministry will shift from your own role and activity to those who provide care to others.

This change is difficult and uncomfortable for most leaders, because they are forever being asked to stand in front of a group. For preachers the temptations of the limelight are even stronger, because their parishioners invariably comment on their performance.

Although being an entertainer is quite different from being a mobilizer, effective preachers do know how to entertain. They understand how to vary their rate, rhythm, volume, and emotional intensity to keep an audience alert. They have mastered the art of holding the attention of an audience.

But performance abilities alone usually cannot grow a church. You may keep the audience in stitches, but if you have set no goals toward which the troops are being mobilized, and no organizational channel has been created for dividing the labor, the church will have a hard time going anywhere.

Self-Evaluation Moment

Think of a recent time that you spoke publicly at church. Which of the following statements represent how you felt afterward?

1. I hope I hear a compliment so I'll know whether or not they liked it.

2. I feel like I gave them a good handle on how to trust God in such-and-such an area.

3. I bet they noticed that I went a few minutes longer than usual.

4. I made such a hero of Katie Kutcel that I bet the crisis-counseling clinic will be flooded with volunteers.

5. I wonder if, in my rush to say everything, I spoke so fast that they couldn't understand everything I said.

Based on your answers, how does the concept of entertainment influence your speaking? How does it motivate to mobilize?

Must Your Church Grow to Please God?

Am I saying that every reader of this book has been called by God to lead more people than he or she is ministering to at present?

No. I have no right to make that kind of statement to anyone. Nothing in this book implies that you must build a larger church or spin off daughter churches if you wish to be fully pleasing to your Lord.

My intent, then, is not to induce false guilt. Nor do I suggest any shortcuts to know God and wait on his leading. The only "must" I offer is the need to obey God.

I am certain, however, that God's will for his kingdom involves numerical growth. Many of you, through your prayer life and sensitivity to the Holy Spirit, have the suspicion that God wants to use you as part of that larger work. As such, you are looking for the tools and perspectives necessary to accomplish this larger agenda. It is to such a growth bias that this chapter speaks.

Almost ten thousand church leaders have participated in the "How to Break the 200 Barrier" seminar offered through the Charles E. Fuller Institute of Evangelism and Church Growth.[2] The two-hundred-persons church faces a growth hurdle that stymies four out of five North American churches.[3]

From the research conducted both during and after these conferences, we have discovered a number of significant facts. First, most seminar attenders had a desire before they came to the event to break a barrier (whether it was 50, 100, 200, or 250). Afterward, 93 percent either agreed or strongly agreed that they left the conference more inspired and encouraged to break their particular growth ceiling and in better possession of the technical knowledge necessary to do so.

The experience at the seminar, then, both strengthened their resolve and caused them to say, "I have the technical knowledge I need." When asked which elements of the technical know-how were most fruitful, the alumni invariably gave high ranking to the shepherd-rancher principle.

Second, two-thirds of these alumni reported actual increases in their churches' growth that were larger than could be attributed to seasonal fluctuation. This number is probably low, because the survey included some people who had not been away from the seminar long enough to be able to put their ideas into practice. The actual figure may be 75 percent of alumni who saw increases.

What do we learn from these findings? Church growth can happen, but not simply because of technique. It is more a matter of heart first and then of having a certain level of technique.

> A growth bias, then, stems more from vision than from ministry style. Church growth is more a matter of heart first and then of having a certain level of technique.

It May Feel Funny

Part of that vision involves what the business community calls the move from being a worker to being a manager. That is, the manager's responsibility is to see to it that the job gets done, whether or not the manager has a hands-on role.

This conceptual leap can be difficult, because it may not feel right. I introduced this chapter by referring to how the leader's sense of worth is sometimes tied up in the strokes he or she receives while actually doing primary-care ministry: the bedside, the counseling, even the sermon. Some things, like the sermon, usually cannot be delegated, nor can a number of certain hospital calls, such as those to powerful or long-time members who more or less demand that the senior pastor visit them.

Many leaders will feel awkward trying to get far enough away from the day-to-day ministry to be able to conceptualize this new paradigm: that people need care, but the clergy are not the only persons who ought to provide this care and, in fact, perhaps should not invest as much time in offering solo primary care as in leadership development.

In addition, sometimes parishioners feel uncomfortable with the shift. They expect their clergy to be available. They may even try to pressure the pastor back into the sheepherder mold.

Chuck Swindoll, senior minister of First Evangelical Free Church, Fullerton, California, a church of more than six thousand people, once described to me the personal pain he experienced during such a transition.

On one occasion, a long-term Sunday school leader came to Mr. Swindoll and said, "Pastor, the last two years, when I invited you to our Sunday school Christmas party, you turned me down. This year I'm not going to take no for an answer. You have to come."

Pastor Swindoll said that the encounter hit a painful nerve. Everything inside him wanted to say yes to this friend.

Instead, he replied, "I turned you down the last two years for the same reason I'm going to turn you down today, and any future year you ask. We now have twenty adult Bible fellowships, all of which have Christmas parties, and if I attend those parties, the Swindoll family will not have Christmas. There would be too much going on. So I've had to decline all invitations, and I hope you can come to terms with that decision."

I could feel Pastor Swindoll's pain as he told how the Sunday school leader walked away in an angry huff. Pastor Swindoll knew that overextending himself further would cause more long-term harm than good. But it still hurt. He told me that it somehow felt terribly wrong to say no to a member who expected the senior pastor to be available.

Was the Sunday school class really less cared for because the senior pastor did not attend? No. For serious needs, the church has numerous recovery groups and counselors, both lay and professional, on referral for every kind of purpose imaginable.

What about the class's social and fellowship needs? The very gentleman who demanded Pastor Swindoll's attendance was doing an excellent job of providing care for that fifty-or-so-person meeting and was organizing parties all year long. He merely wanted a special treat for his class. He thought that by doing some foot stamping and showing a little edge of belligerency, perhaps he could win for his group what the others had not been able to achieve: the special attention of the senior pastor.

The fact is that no one suffered because of the pastor's absence at the party. The only distress present was inside the member who expected that his senior pastor would, in fact, do all the personal ministry himself, and inside the pastor who wished he could but found himself unable to do so.

Here is a fact many pastors must face: The more inclined the pastor is toward direct personal involvement, the greater is his or her struggle learning to see to it that ministry is done as opposed to doing the ministry alone.

Only by vision can such a hurdle be overcome.

The Inner Turmoil

What is the next development that shapes the vision of someone who wants to lead a flock through the dependency-on-the-clergy barrier and its accompanying limited size?

The vision components are similar in every barrier situation, whether the threshold is two hundred, two thousand, or twenty thousand. The leader will recognize where the church is, how it came to be there, and what it needs to do to reach a goal beyond.

This perspective translates itself into an ever present concern that human beings are desperately in need of having the love of God mediated to them in personal terms. An accompanying passion says that the community of the redeemed, left at its present size, will fall far short of what Jesus Christ would like to accomplish through them.

As that pairing of images permeates the soul of the visionary pastor, the images flesh themselves out through such statements as, "I must commission others to see to it that this work is done, even though certain dear saints, without realizing it, want to limit the growth of the kingdom by restricting care to the personal strength and resources that I as a minister can bring to bear."

What propels a church leader to keep moving forward like that? What can create a "champion" church that accepts and encourages new paradigms of ministry? I believe the answer involves a joining together of both vision and skill.

My son Bob is a discus thrower. When he first started, he could barely make 100 feet. As his coaches worked with him, his throw moved from 100 to 105 to 110 to 120 to 130. When he finished his high school career he was hurling nearly 150 feet. He had constantly raised his standard.

Bob's senior-year coach, an athlete who could throw 200 feet and more, trained Bob by working out with him. They would say, "Here's where we are. What can we do to exceed that?"

With Bob, as with church leaders, there was a combination of technical proficiencies and an issue of heart. One fuels the other, and the net result is that barriers are broken.

Furthermore, in most fields of high accomplishment, mentors, trainers, and models are part of the picture. Champion salesmen seek out other winning salespersons. Champion students seek out other master scholars. People put themselves alongside each other and stretch each other.

We have learned, at the Charles E. Fuller Institute, that the pastors who are going to make it in church growth are ones no one has to chase to teach about church growth. They select themselves for breaking barriers, because they dare to dream and imagine that there is a better future out there than the one they have experienced.

The Most Important Growth Bias

I submit that the most important issue in empowerment is a holy imagination of what God can lead a person to become. I believe that in the formation of this sanctified self-image, a Christian can perceive him- or herself as a person who will benefit others by associating with them.

> The most important issue in empowerment is a holy imagination of what God can lead a person to become.

This view is not some exaggerated notion of a prideful self. Rather, it stems from the notion that my adequacy comes from a relationship of walking with Christ, and that what I offer to others is provided by an overflow of what I have received from the person of Christ himself. Jesus said (to paraphrase John 15:4–8), "If you hope to do my will you will have to abide in me. If you will abide in me, you will bear fruit in your life."

The privilege of being a person who becomes a positive benefit to others is not based on a magnificent character, nor on sinless perfection, nor on high intelligence. Rather, this sense of adequacy springs from staying connected to the person of Jesus Christ. All I need do is let his Word abide in me and consciously depend on his sufficiency.

I can speak from experience on what it means to run dry. During one period of my life a pressing schedule and frustrating realization of the yet-unreached harvest led me to a point of such dryness that I felt like an engine running in overheat that had run out of oil.

I found myself so frustrated, dismayed, and angry, so dry and despairing, that one dear friend stopped me and said, "Carl, it is a sin to despair."

He was right. I had looked at the needs so apparent all around me and had thought I was responsible for meeting them all.

Ultimately I confessed, "God, *I* know that I am not adequate, and *you* know that I am not adequate. Now that we've got the facts straight, how about giving me some of your adequacy here for the task ahead?"

Yet I still held on, thinking I needed to do something to make the difference. I kept using my own strength. I remember driving to a seminar I was to lead. On my way, I held an exhausting conversation on the car phone. A colleague in another state was wrestling with issues so charged that the emotions leaped across the airwaves. I could feel the energy drain out of me.

I could have said, "I have to give a speech in a few minutes and need some time to refresh myself." But I hung up the phone, noticed that the last bit of energy had left my soul, walked into the conference room completely empty, and started speaking anyway.

The next hour and a half was one of the worst of my life. The haunting failure that occurred when I tried to offer inspiration to a group of people, when I had no emotional or spiritual cushion, is a painful memory I will never forget.

In fact, I hope to remember it for this simple reason: The experience was entirely preventable. Had I taken just a few minutes, sung together with the group, prayed with them, spent time in quiet before the Lord, admitted my emptiness, and confessed my need of the Lord's presence, that consulting session would have been redeemed. And the fruit of it would still be apparent today.

What a contrast between that event and the empowerment that could have come from on high! Where was the holy imagination that affirms that a believer can be a channel of the grace of God? That the Christian's very presence gives something that cannot be had otherwise? That the redeemed person is valued not because of a sweet personality, and not because of a great smile, but because in his or her presence Jesus has the freedom to be present, too?

> The redeemed person is valued because in his or her presence Jesus has the freedom to be present, too.

The God we serve is the kind who takes unlikely people and makes something beautiful of them. God tells the readers and writer of this book, "You can do it!" In the kingdom of God, unlikely people turn out to be astonishing performers.

Had someone analyzed the apostles Peter or Paul just after their conversions, the conclusion might have been, "You'll probably not become anything significant." Yet God used these two unusual people to turn the whole Roman Empire upside down.

If you are a growing Christian, stationed where he wants you to serve, you probably have the capacity to project a growth bias to your people. God can use your encouragement to affirm to your people that he wants to do something special through them.

What would happen if, in the next meeting you lead, you purpose not to use one word of scolding, or even of busying the church with the status quo? What if, instead, you say, "I'm looking at a group of champions. I'm talking to people who can be developed into a victorious army for God."

Or, if you do pulpit ministry, why not spend some of your preparation time imagining how your message will empower your laity for significant ministry? Preach not to the rebellious but to those who have said "yes" to God and want to go forward.

Have you ever noticed that some sports coaches, no matter where they move around the country, and no matter what the previous records of the ball clubs they currently lead, can produce championship teams?

True, these coaches do tend to attract good players. But there is more. They possess a quality that brings a winning vision to what they are doing.

Your pulpit could be the end of the bench in the locker room at halftime in the big game. What the coach says is not very important compared with what the players do when they go back on the field.

> What the coach says is not very important compared with what the players do when they go back on the field.

The nature of oratorical preaching puts the spotlight on you. In response, you need to swing that spotlight around and say, "Look folks, you are the real stars. The quality of my sermons is not nearly as important as how well your children are turning out. Don't tell me how many times you've been here in the service; instead, talk to me about how you cut off the television and spent time with your spouse praying for the salvation of your neighbors."

Coaching is attitudinal. It contains technical elements, but you will get the technique if you stay with it.

So is leading a church. When I was an intern in the ministry, just after graduate school, my pastor had a favorite saying as he went to work with people. He would say, "You know, you're a part of this formula. Whether or not you think you can, you're right!"

The same applies to the climate of your church. Do you have a growth bias? Do you truly believe God will enlarge the scope of your church's harvest? Whether or not you think you can, you're right.

For Further Thought

1. Do you agree with the opening comments about performance, entertainment, and mobilizing? Why or why not? What Scripture verses either challenge or affirm each of these motives?

2. Look again at the section "Must Your Church Grow to Please God?" Do you think God calls all churches to numerical growth? What other kinds of spiritual maturation could take place in a church without being accompanied by eventual numerical growth?

3. How did you feel about how Chuck Swindoll responded to the Sunday school member? Would you have handled it any differently? Have you ever participated in or observed a similar experience?

4. Review the section about abiding in Christ and depending on his sufficiency. What makes the difference between someone who is arrogant and someone who exudes the grace of God?

5. If you are a preacher, do you believe there is any connection between your reward in heaven and your homiletic ability? Would you be pressing the issue too far if you said that God's greatest interest in your message is whether you present your sermon in such a way that your people are moved to obey God?

PART 2

Learn How
to Ranch

6

Why Develop the Skills
of a Rancher?

In a church in which I was pastor, one of our members was a butcher, a massive, muscled man who had once been a professional football player. He was diagnosed with leukemia and, in the course of three weeks, died.

My job, as the "professional," was to break the news to his two little boys. The experience tore me apart. I sat there looking at the boys and realized that absolutely nothing I could say, even though I was a trained clergyman, would make a difference. How could I tell them that Daddy loved them, Mommy loved them, Jesus loved them, and the preacher loved them, but that Daddy would not be coming home again?

The best thing I could do, I decided, would be to stop at their house every afternoon and play baseball with them. How long, though, would my church board tolerate that?

To make matters worse, I watched helplessly as their mother struggled through a remarriage which failed. As their family life unraveled, those boys became like orphans.

I continued to feel helpless and guilty. I was their pastor, their shepherd. My job was to provide care and meet their needs, was it not?

During those times of feeling inadequate, I would pray, "God, help me! Even if it takes all my life, I've got to find a better solution. My running over to their house for various crises, offering up a blessing, and then driving away, is producing little, if any, lasting good."

After almost two decades, I am convinced that I have found what was missing. What the boys needed was a community of extended family, akin to those in the frontier days when aunts, uncles, and close caring neighbors made sure that everything would be in place for the boys to receive the nurture they needed—from hugs and listening ears to baseball gloves and food on the table.

The first step in my twenty-year journey toward a more whole perspective was to identify myself as a sheepherder and then question whether that role was truly what God calls a pastor to be.

This chapter will, in part, describe myself in my younger years and the literally thousands of fellow sheepherders whom I have observed, counseled with, and researched over the years.

Foundation for Ranching

I do not criticize the role of a shepherd. I am, however, laying the foundation for my conviction that the concept of pastor needs a broader, fuller definition than that of sheepherder if we are truly to *multiply* disciples, as Jesus commanded in his Great Commission (Matt. 28:19–20).

I will go one step further: Maybe the common stereotype of what it means to be a pastor is an imbalanced view. Yes, Jesus does talk about himself as the Good Shepherd who "calls his own sheep by name" (John 10:3), and who says, "Take care of my sheep" (John 21:16). Many clergy extrapolate that image to mean that the ideal pastor will know each parishioner personally and be available whenever one of those sheep has a need.

But that represents only a portion of the biblical imperative for a church leader and, frankly, may be applicable only to Christ, the one and only Chief Shepherd (1 Peter 5:4). After all, the only one truly capable of being all-knowing and omnipresent is God.

What about such scriptural terms as *overseer* (Acts 20:28; 1 Tim. 3:2; Titus 1:7) or *leader* (Heb. 13:7; 13:17)? In the listings of spiritual gifts, can pastors (or shepherds) be endowed by the Holy Spirit with gifts of "leadership" (Rom. 12:8) or "gifts of administration"

(1 Cor. 12:28)? If so, is there more to or something different in a pastor's role than staying nose to nose with all the sheep?

Similarly, what are the pastoral implications of the numerous texts that encourage a mutual "building up" of the body (Eph. 4:12–13, 29; Rom. 15:2; 1 Cor. 3:1–15; 14:12; 2 Cor. 10:8; 13:10; Col. 2:7; 1 Thess. 5:11)? Is it not curious that Paul, in describing pastoral care, uses the image of shepherd only once (Eph. 4:11), and instead employs a wide range of terminology such as *steward of Christ, teacher, example, priest,* and *helmsman?*[1]

How about Jesus' pattern of leadership development (as analyzed in *The Disciple Making Pastor*[2] and elsewhere)? In my opinion, his approach to "sheep" was much more the model of the rancher than the sheepherder.

As you read through the following, ask yourself which perspectives best represent the overall teachings of Scripture and the pattern Jesus followed. Also, mull over the implications for size. What correlation do you observe between the leadership style that seems most suited for a numerically plateaued church of fifty and that most suited for a growing church of one hundred?

Push your imagination further by asking what kind of personality is needed to pastor a church of five hundred, one thousand, five thousand, ten thousand, or fifty thousand. If you think these numbers are too high, think of how many unchurched people are within a fifteen-minute drive of your place of worship. What if, through a great awakening akin to other revival periods in American history, these people all began to hunger for spiritual nurture? Would your church be able to service their spiritual needs?

Self-Evaluation Moment

1. Which words best describe how you feel right now about the concept of rancher: curious, hesitant, confused, a bit defensive, fearful, eager?

2. How do you feel about the biblical underpinnings of the rancher idea: intrigued, unconvinced, encouraged, neutral, surprised, reluctant?

How Sheepherders Behave

Our field observations indicate that 90 to 95 percent of pastors begin their ministry as sheepherders. Following are their most common characteristics. Remember, what they do is not wrong; I focus on their behavior, not their hearts.

1. Primary caregiving. Sheepherding pastors try to be the major care providers for the entire church. When they come across a need they ask, "How will *I* meet it?"

When they ask themselves who the adequate caregivers are, they, like Elijah (see 1 Kings 19:14), feel they are probably the only ones, or at least the best ones.

2. Overestimated significance. The spotlight on their crisis intervention, hospital calls, and other pastoral acts prevents their seeing the support roles that are essential to effective care.

It is one thing to tell a church member that her husband has died. It is another for friends and relatives to live with that widow through the two years of grieving that she needs to surrender her spouse to death.

The true care heroes are those who supply the enormous amounts of required aftercare.

3. Expectation drivenness. Sheepherders attempt to meet all expectations by being omnipresent. They feel bound to attend every committee meeting or program lest they hear the disappointing news, "It just wasn't the same without you" (meaning, "You've created a dependency syndrome").

"What do my people expect of me?" and "Am I measuring up?" are their constant driving motivations. As a result, people set the agenda for the pastors rather than that the pastors set the cadence for the march.

4. Availability. They think in terms of how they can be more accessible to the church. Such ministers convey to the church that they will be available for whatever is necessary.

I remember the first time I heard a pastor refuse to be available for a parishioner's funeral. I thought it an ungodly attitude. He was preaching fifty funerals a year and was headed out for a much-needed vacation with his family. He said, "Although I will not be here for the funeral and cannot come back from the beach, my associate will conduct the funeral in accordance with the departed one's wishes. Let me pray with you before God. I will see you when I return." And he left town.

I thought, *How irresponsible and uncaring can you be?* I was operating on the principle that says, "Even if it means interrupting my vacation I will come back and be here so that your dependence on me will be secured."

Many problems in the parsonage stem from this attitude. Being ever on call means being less available to one's own family. The situation is as if the pastor has a mistress called the church and gives the family the leftovers. The wife is at a disadvantage in trying to cope with a husband who has these characteristics, unless she also is a sheepherder by disposition.

If she has a different personality, she is likely to feel mad as a hornet. "If he were literally fooling around on me, I'd confront him," she says. "But what can I do when the church is my competition?"

So she is stuck. The choices are to be angry with her husband, be angry with God, or be self-reproachful. The despair frequently found in the manse stems from a wife who has decided to turn her anger on herself and lives in a brooding condition of self-disrespect, shame, and guilt. (I will expand on this topic in chapter 8.)

5. Performance. Sheepherders almost seem to think, How can I keep them from getting along without me? Although they do not actually verbalize these thoughts, their behavior indicates it.

Their motto tends to be, Watch me assure these hospital patients that I'll be back soon. In other words, Watch me do ministry.

Because their attention is riveted on this kind of performance, the strokes they hunger for are linked to their performance standards. They regularly reflect on how the people like their sermons and if the people are pleased with their bedside manners.

6. Role comfort. Although sheepherders work to the limit of their time and energy, they do not ask for a greater vision than what they can do by themselves. They may be tired, but they are happy: "I'm so grateful to be needed!"

I remember many a time going home dead tired. As I would lie down in bed I would say, "Isn't it wonderful to be this tired and this happy, because I was needed every hour today?"

Never mind that my wife would say, "What about my needs? What about our children's needs? What about the needs of others in the church who haven't been given the chance to develop the same kind of serving skills you so enjoy?"

Years passed before I finally understood the reason behind the incongruence between my perspective and my wife's. Much of my activity had stemmed from a need to prove that I was worthy and worthwhile.

Sheepherders experience role comfort when they behave consistently, whether effectively or not. They are comfortable, because they live a ritualized life. In their liturgies of economy, efficiency, and consistency, they avoid uncomfortable questions about whether a different path would lead to greater effectiveness.

> Sheepherders avoid uncomfortable questions about whether a different path would lead to greater effectiveness.

7. Poor delegating ability. When sheepherders delegate, they tend to specify methods, not outcomes. If a lay volunteer comes along who is more effectiveness oriented, this person becomes frustrated, because the level of directions is more in terms of how the pastor would do it rather than of measurable outcomes. In addition, sheepherders require constant approval of projects in terms of how something is done rather than what is being done, whether or not such feedback is appropriate or necessary.

Progress becomes bottlenecked, because sheepherders fail to fulfill a manager's role; they are too busy keeping the work close to themselves. They attract people who are willing to forward the pastor's agenda rather than contribute their own, people who have the gift of helps or of hospitality: "Can I join with you on this, Pastor?" or, "How can I help you, Pastor?"

Pretty soon such pastors lament the fact that nobody is present with skills beyond those of hanging up coats and opening doors.

If these sheepherders do use administratively gifted people, they position them primarily as advisors to themselves: "If you were me, what would you advise that I do?" So the advice they hear is usually in keeping with a sheepherder's innocuousness.

8. Poor planning. If they do plan, it's en route to doing. They are frequently caught in an activity cycle: "Here I am again. By the way, what am I going to do?" They find they are too committed to their processes to be able to achieve their overall goals more efficiently or more effectively.

Their inadequate planning leads to a shortfall of help which, in turn, leads to their doing ministry by themselves. Caught in such a cycle, they regularly bypass the milestones at which others might join the work.

9. Individualism. They tend to see the church as made up of individual members. Thus, rather than visualize ministry through the perspective of a work force, they perceive it as something to be negotiated through their relationships with specific persons.

10. Ignorance of trends. Shepherds live in the now of experience. Their assessment of how things are going derives more from whether they experienced any disagreeable encounters in the last few hours than from reflection on worship trends, giving patterns, or achievement of church goals.

They do not easily correlate forecasts with needed action. They sit, waiting and watching as changes occur but unaware of their significance, because they are so busy ministering nose to nose with the sheep.

The greatest blind spot of most sheepherders is their lack of a sense of growth history and attendance tracking. Why? For sheepherders to take attendance implies that they might have control of it or responsibility for it.

The sheepherder finds it easier to say, "It's God's business to bless, and if he chooses to bless, fine, and if not, fine."

Did not Jesus also say things like, "Whatever *you* bind on earth will be bound in heaven, and whatever *you* loose on earth will be loosed in heaven" (Matt. 16:19, emphasis added)? Yet, sheepherders would rather trade in the unseeable spiritual realities than in the measurable organizational realities.

How Ranchers Behave

By contrast, the rancher gives greater and more careful attention to organizational needs than to personal and professional needs, as seen in these characteristics (also summarized in Figure 4):

Figure 4

Are You a Sheepherder?

1. Primary Caregiving
2. Overestimated Significance
3. Expectation Drivenness
4. Availability
5. Performance
6. Role Comfort
7. Poor Delegating Ability
8. Poor Planning Ability
9. Individualism
10. Ignorance of Trends

Or a Rancher?

1. Emphasis on the Big Picture
2. Take-Charge Competence
3. One-Another Ministry Expectation
4. Group Focus
5. Flexible Supervision
6. Outcome Objectives
7. Large-Picture Focus
8. Role Creation
9. Nondependency
10. Managerial Skills

© 1992 Carl F. George

1. Emphasis on the big picture. The rancher may seem not to need people or to be indifferent to their problems.

In reality, however, ranchers are so concerned about people's needs that they are unwilling to abandon themselves to the concerns of the ninety-nine while they search for the one. Ranching, they believe, represents the best way to achieve God's purposes for the entire flock.

Ranchers make sure the flock receives pastoral care in a measurable way, primarily through systems of nonclergy-dependent, mutual self-care.[3] The typical forum for this kind of one-another nurture is a small group of eight to thirteen people (to be discussed in chapters 9 through 12).

2. Take-charge competence. Ranchers set expectations much as a band director sets the tempo for the song. This trait particularly shows up in areas of change and confrontation.

For example, suppose a single person in the church is living in an unmarried state with another person. The sheepherder says, "What am I supposed to do? My board members are so tolerant of sin that they wouldn't assist or back me if I tried to initiate disciplinary measures."

The rancher takes a different tack. "Before I attempt to discipline this individual, I'd better get the board in shape. If there's any shacking up going on in their own lives, I'd better have that already worked out so that they can deal credibly with problems like this."

So the rancher sets the terms for being on the board. "We're going to pray together, study the Bible together, work together, and obey God together. If this isn't to your liking, then maybe a board role is not the best place of service for you at this church."

The rancher knows how to put the board through an intense training time to promote the spirituality and leadership skills of the people on the board, so that when they complete their time on the board they can be more effective ministers from that point on.

No pastor can bring about such changes overnight. But the improvements will never happen unless the pastor knows how to start calling certain shots.

3. One-another ministry expectation. Ranchers set the expectations that the members of the church will give and receive care

among one another. A rancher will hold up this standard in such a way that everyone understands this is how they do it.

Churches are partly intentional societies and mostly folk cultures governed by a fabric of unwritten rules and expectations. One steering mechanism in folk cultures is the hero making that occurs in the process of telling stories (as described in chapter 3). The rancher publicly cheers those role models who show the way ministry "ought" to be done. The rancher sets up a system of mutual care so that the little "ow-ees," emergency calls, and crises that occur weekly do not prevent him or her from attending to the greater works that God wants done.

4. Group focus. Ranchers perceive the church in terms of objectives, groups, and ministry teams. Gatherings call for leaders, and teams need supervisors. Ranchers, grasping this concept, view their work not as relationships with individuals but as objectives to be accomplished and a staff to be supervised. Acting like the site manager of a huge construction project, they say, "To get this job done, we need two teams for this and three groups for that."

Therefore, the rancher sends people, not one by one—because they would require continual maintenance and nurture—but team by team, so that they can keep themselves nurtured, maintained, and high in morale.

Ranchers see the church, in other words, in terms of group life. When they find administratively gifted persons, ranchers use such persons as program organizers rather than simply as advisors to themselves.

If they ask, "What would you recommend that I do about this situation?" they do not imply, What should *I* do about it? but, What do you recommend needs to be blessed and done about it?

They know how to change the focus of the work from themselves to the objective of the organization, to be owned by the organization. The rancher responds, "That sounds like the prescription we need; we'll implement that. Are you willing to take a part in it? If so, take your prescription and work it out. If not, we'll hand your prescription to someone who is willing.

5. Flexible supervision. Therefore, ranchers delegate work and then supervise others. To be effective they must learn enough flexi-

bility in delegation style to meet the needs of persons willing to receive the assignments.

For example, entrepreneurial personalities need only the go-ahead to do the ministry. They are independent initiative takers. All the rancher has to say is, "Here's how what you're doing supports our vision, here's your access to resources, and here's how we'll know when the job is properly done. Please avoid such-and-such, and check back with me to report progress at such-and-such a point."

Other types of people cannot simply take an order and run with it. They have to sit and nurse through a problem and visualize it in the presence of a group of concerned people until they have drawn out all the issues—quality assurances, misgivings, subtleties, and preferences. These kinds of persons often love to sit and plan. They would prefer four hours of planning to one hour of execution. Then they need to come back and celebrate that accomplishment before taking on something new.

If you try to treat both types of people similarly, you will achieve greater success mixing oil and water. I will further address the issue of delegation in chapter 10.

6. Outcome objectives. Ranchers focus on what something will look like when it is complete, not how to get there. They are open to ethical, legitimate ways of getting something done that they themselves have not thought of yet. For the rancher, something being "my idea" is not a precondition for the acceptability of the method.

Ranchers appreciate those who have appropriate gifts for the position. Whereas the sheepherder appreciates comfort from those with the gifts of helps and hospitality, the rancher appreciates the fact that the giftedness of laypeople will be broad enough to do the variety of things that God wishes to have done.

7. Large-picture focus. Ranchers screen requests for their services by asking two questions: Is this the kind of thing our church ought to be doing, and by whom should it best be done?

What if the ministry opportunity seems important, and after all resources have been exhausted it seems the rancher will need to become involved? The rancher, before jumping in, hesitates and says, "If I'm the one to do it, maybe it shouldn't be done at all."

Everyone in ministry, whatever the style, struggles with passing up an opportunity for fear of missing something that may take the church into the future. But there comes a point in the rancher's life when the rancher realizes, energy must be conserved for what is strategically most important: keeping the entire ranch running smoothly. If I become distracted by this opportunity, knowing that not all opportunities are necessarily godsends, am I going to be able to do all the other things that need to get done?

8. Role creation. Ranchers also create roles and they will fill those roles, assigning the jobs or delegating them to other people. They know how job maturity affects the type of support needed. In other words, if someone is doing something for the first time and is insecure in the process, that person will need a different kind of attention than one who has done it several times.

Furthermore, ranchers will recognize the differences in the types of support needed. Does the person need feedback such as, "You are so gifted. This is going to make the folks at the soup kitchen feel encouraged"? Or is the worker more instructional and task oriented, requiring comments such as, "Here are the techniques you can use"?

Furthermore, as people start jobs they need instructions. Later on, they need a little patting. After a while, they can get along without instructions if they receive occasional notice. Ultimately, they will do their ministry whether the rancher has a role in it or not, because the intrinsic value of the activity is payoff enough for them. Their main concern about the pastor at that point is that he or she not get in their way.

9. Nondependency. The driving motivation of a rancher is how to enable people to function well without the pastor. One of the rancher's solutions is to affirm people's talents: "Bless you. You do a great job with that!"

When someone challenges the rancher's apparent loss of control, the rancher does not feel defensive or threatened. "No, this person's willingness to minister means that lives are being touched, even if I am at home getting some much-needed rest." Ranchers' freedoms originate in a mental permission note they carry around:

> Dear Friend,
>   You do not have to carry the burden of the whole world today. That's my job.
>   Love,
>   God

Ranchers refuse to live on the schedule of a nursing mother, who can allow her baby to be away only so many minutes between feedings and changings. Ranchers want their spiritual offspring to grow up—or at least to be nursed by someone else—so they can think, pray, and plan the next hill that the church, as a whole, needs to climb.

10. Managerial skills. Most pastors have learned managerial talk; few have developed the competence of managerial behavior. Pulpit ministers, in general, are articulate. They are experts at sounding good. They excel at appearing to be fully adequate.

The reality? When ministers speak of their dreams, I pause at the part that sounds slickest and without hitches. I begin to probe those areas. It inevitably turns out that the more ideal-sounding the plan, the less the minister knows about how to pull it off.

Ranchers reserve solitude time for planning and prayer. They make planning a formal, written activity, even if they minister in a context where everything has to be announced orally. They develop skills to sense needs, define problems, and solve problems.

When to Make the Shift

Can shepherds become ranchers? Frequently, if they want to. Unless such pastors are convinced that they are fulfilling all God is calling them to become, I urge them to carefully and incrementally revise their behavior in favor of a more effective set of skills, feelings, perceptions, and behaviors.

What about a church that is small? Should the leaders wait to develop pastoral ranching skills until the fellowship shows some growth?

No. For any size church to grow, the leader must address the management issues related to ranching. Otherwise, the church may betray the growth opportunities sent to it.

In almost every case, small-parish pastors think of their churches as smaller than they actually are. They do not realize that the church needs a better organizational scheme or more deliberate supervisory skills.

In preparing a church for growth, the first person to deal with in the chain of change is the minister, because he or she sets up a community of self-reinforcement that either assures nongrowth or permits growth.

Must You Develop Rancher Skills?

Some pastors and lay leaders serve churches that, like a poodle, seem to follow them around wherever they go. The people do not attempt much of anything without them. If the leader is not there, everything goes on hold. Both pastor and church find great comfort in the sheepherder role.

Such an experience is not limited to smaller churches. Many people, even in larger churches, are mentally and emotionally back at the level of a lap-dog church.[4]

I cannot tell you God's will for your particular situation. Maybe you are already ministering to everyone he wants to bring your way. Maybe the circumstances are such that your context is best served by a sheepherder. As I pointed out in chapter 5, you must make that decision before God.

In counseling with pastors and lay leaders, I find that sometimes their motivation to stay at their present level stems from an unmet need on their part. Some sheepherders enjoy feeling indispensable because of personal workaholism, a need to control others or to be treated like deity to feel good, or a need to be a big fish in a little pond. I will further discuss these tendencies in chapter 8.

Why Ranching Is Significant

What's the bottom line on these two ministry styles? People's need to receive care must exceed your need to give it. If you are to be effective in ministry, you must accept the fact that there will be times when you cannot be both available and adequate.[5]

I suggest that by shifting paradigms pastors or lay leaders can help more people than they would have previously thought possible. In faithfulness to God they say, "We're here as your instruments of your gospel, of your kingdom, of your body, and we want to do all you are calling us to do in this place."

Therefore, what if God wanted you to handle twice as many people as you are ministering to at present? What if there are people in your church whom God wants to bless, but because you are sticking with a limited way of doing things, you cannot turn those people loose to find God's blessing?

> What if God wanted you to handle twice as many people as you are ministering to at present?

I do not believe I have the right to impose a particular growth rate or church size on someone else. But I do believe I have an obligation to encourage pastors and lay leaders to ask God if he might be interested in touching more people than they have previously imagined.

I have yet to be in a place where, from everything I could sense, God was not more willing to bless than the leaders were willing to receive. God wants to give you a spiritually healthy church with a positive, faith-oriented, biblically sound approach to your community, under Christ, such that if someone joins you, he or she will be significantly better off for having done so.

Maybe that means touching ten more people than at present. Or maybe it means ten thousand. Your responsibility is to do whatever you can, humanly speaking, to make spiritual ministry available for "whosoever will."

And, in my opinion, the rancher style is the most effective way to multiply the scope of your ministry.

For Further Thought

1. Which sheepherder characteristics describe your ministry style? Which rancher characteristics? How are you different today, in this regard, from the way you were a year ago?

2. In the history of your particular church, would you say the sheepherder style or the rancher style has been more predominant? Why? What factors influence your church either to desire sheepherders or to tolerate ranchers?

3. The section of this chapter "Foundation for Ranching" mentions a number of biblical terms, images, and directives. Which statement is the most eye-opening to you? Which angle would you like to pursue further? Why?

4. Respond to these statements: What's the bottom line on these two ministry styles? People's need to receive care must exceed your need to give it. There will be times when you cannot be both available and adequate.

5. If you operated more like a rancher, in what ways would your church be different one year from now? five years from now?

7

Where Do You Stand on the Sheepherder-Rancher Spectrum?

During my early pastoral years, I ministered as if the world's salvation hung on my being available for everyone's primary-care needs. Through my preaching, church-staff supervision, church-school administration, and being on call for twenty-four-hour hospital visitation, I conveyed the idea that I was glad to take care of any situation just as soon as I could get there.

If someone had asked why my ministry was so dependency centered, I would have responded with a blank stare. I was grateful to be needed! I had a churchful of people who viewed me as their shepherd. What greater sign of effectiveness could I want?

Coaching Instead of Doing

One year, however, as I was busy wearing myself out, a certain church member began to outpersist me in hospital visitation. She continually embarrassed me by being at the bedside before I could get there. Each time she gave me a report on her "rounds," I was stung by my inability to effectively cover the territory. My feelings of guilt prevented me from seeing how much this woman delighted in her daily search to find and minister to a different sick person.

If this were not enough, another parishioner began handing me prospect cards on all the people she met. She seemed to come across a new person every two hours. My desk at work and dresser at home were soon buried under these cards, and all I could think of was how inadequate I was.

This frustrating overload drove me to ask a strange question. On a particular Sunday, when I saw one of these dear saints walking toward me with news of yet another contact, I became angry at the increased work she generated for me. I looked at her and thought, "What on earth has made you so caring?"

An answer from heaven instantly entered my mind: "*I* made her that way, so don't you despise what you see."

"If that's what you've done," I shot back to God, "then what am I supposed to do?"

The Lord then impressed me with an idea that I have used for more than two decades. I decided to coach this lady on how to do the ministry by herself or along with another layperson.

"If you were to go for me," I explained when she again recruited me for a new hospital need, "you might select a passage of Scripture, read it, say a prayer for the person, and ask if things are well with his soul." As I continued this impromptu training session, I quickly discovered that she seemed able to learn to present the plan of salvation as capably as I.

Even so, I was still terrified as I spoke. I was about to give away a role that most ordained people, including myself, have traditionally insisted on fulfilling themselves. I was giving ministry to an unlicensed and unordained person who had nothing but a heart for people and a willingness to be taught. Could she really pull this off without as much training as I had had? Somehow, I proceeded to encourage and authorize her to do the ministry. As she walked away, I suspected I had unleashed a dynamic that I would understand much better in the years to come.

That event indeed turned out to be pivotal. It was my first step away from a clergy-dependency mind-set.

Through dozens of similar situations, the Holy Spirit has prompted me to be more effective in directing, managing, and delegating ministry, rather than attempting to do it all myself. I have matured in this area step by step, in things as little as handing some chalk to a leading board member, sitting down, and letting him use his administrative gifts to chart out a change I had proposed.

Learning is always an ongoing, never-ending process. As the ancient proverbs say: "The heart of the discerning acquires knowledge; the ears of the wise seek it out" (Prov. 18:15); and, "Instruct a wise man and he will be wiser still; teach a righteous man and he will add to his learning" (Prov. 9:9).

Your Turn to Ranch

Ranchers are not judged by what they can do themselves. Their value now depends primarily on what they can get done through others. The starting point for action, then, is to spend time training others.

What does the following checklist reveal about how you invested your ministry hours in recent weeks?

Self-Evaluation Moment

Tally, by category, how you spent your "church" energies during the last week (or month).

Hours

_____ preaching or teaching, including preparation time

_____ administration and planning

_____ prayer

_____ visitation and counseling

_____ participation in classes or small groups

_____ supervision of staff or ministry leaders

_____ community, social, or civic events

_____ fellowship with peers, such as fellow clergy

Divide the total number of hours into these two parts:

What percent of your time was spent doing direct, primary-care ministry?_____

What percent of your time was invested in training others for ministry?_____

Is a rancher prohibited from doing hands-on ministry? No. That is the privilege of every believer. But that should be done for free. Rather, I suggest that one way to distinguish the activities of paid, professional clergy is by the fact that the vast majority of their hours go to leadership development.

I challenge pastors to be minister developers, and then to measure every other effect in the church by that standard—not by how impressive is the sermon but by how many ministers are made. Measure not by how available or busy the pastors are but by the extent to which the paid staff contributes to the making of ministers who would care for the constituency and those beyond the constituency in the name of Jesus Christ.

> I challenge pastors to be minister developers, and then to measure every other effect in the church by that standard.

Self-Evaluation Moment

What is wrong with these examples? In each, the leader thinks he or she is ranching. Is that the case?

1. "Michelle, how's it going in that Saturday-morning women's group you started?"

   Close. Better: "Michelle, in that new ladies' group you started, have you decided whom to groom as your apprentice?"

2. "Our final topic for staff meeting is special music for this Sunday. Let's ask Kep and Debbie James to sing. They're our most talented musicians. Shall we ask that trio—Heather, Katie, and Drew—for the next week? Then back to the James's for week three?"

   Probably not. Better: "The Jameses are good musicians and able trainers of others. Let's give them the challenge of producing other music leaders, rather than limiting their role to that of performers."

3. "We need an additional minister who could help me oversee our many new programs."

Maybe. Better: "We need an additional minister who could be responsible for developing lay talent to lead our many new programs."

The question for a rancher to ask himself or herself is, "Am I doing the ministry myself, or am I committing others to do it?" I would go so far as to propose that you should not be doing ministry unless you are modeling or training someone else how to do it. Otherwise, you are merely producing care; you are not increasing your production capabilities. Modeling is legitimate ministry as long as it is witnessed by someone who is going to take responsibility for doing it next. That principle applies to virtually every activity, from fixing the church photocopier to praying for the flock.

Self-Evaluation Moment

What does your prayer life reveal about your position on the sheepherder-rancher spectrum? What kinds of church-related people needs most regularly occupy your prayer times? Check the persons with requests to whom you are most readily drawn:

1. Those whose lives seem to be one crisis after another.
2. Those who have the greatest influence and leadership potential.
3. Those who cause you the most grief.
4. Those who have experienced recent fruit in their ministries.
5. Those with great physical needs.
6. Those who share a passion for ranching.
7. Those parishioners you interact with most frequently, without regard as to whether they play a role in providing care to others.

When one of your parishioners gives you a whole catalog of prayer requests, how are you more likely to respond?

1. Count on me to support you in prayer.

2. Do you have your Bible study (or other small group) praying with you?

Comment: Even-numbered answers tend to be rancher related;
odd numbered are more characteristic of the sheepherder.

The Urgency of the Shift

After almost two decades of careful investigation of the North
American church, it is my growing conviction that the way pastors
manage themselves as church leaders is the single most important
cause for the failure of the churches to perform in the way God
requires and in the way the Holy Spirit would empower them to
accomplish.

Pastors need enough diagnosis to recognize when they are in
trouble and then enough prescription to make a difference when
they set their hearts and minds to a new set of priorities.

> The way pastors manage themselves is the single,
> most important cause for the failure of the churches
> to perform in the way God requires and in the way
> the Holy Spirit would empower them to accomplish.

What is peripheral and what is central? Too many churches lose
valuable ministry energy because their leadership is preoccupied
with that which is marginal to their mission. Even something as
apparently worthwhile as the creation of an in-house training institute that offers an academically oriented, systematic study of the
Bible is, in itself, secondary. Knowledge apart from obedient application does the kingdom of God little good.

What, then, is essential? Those activities that organize a pastor's
time and vision around a system of lay leadership development, so
that greater ministry can be accomplished in ever-widening circles
of influence.

The implications are staggering. If the net result will be that
most churches need far fewer speakers and far more shepherds of
the flock, then the rancher-pastor will need to rethink the role of the

> Knowledge apart from obedient application
> does the kingdom of God little good.

vast majority of a church's meetings. Likewise, the prevalent didactic model for judging ministry will be deemed inappropriate. The current stroking-and-reward patterns—number of cassettes reproduced, number of radio or TV listeners—will prove to be almost irrelevant ways to keep score.

A rancher helps a church to state a goal or a mission statement that is in keeping with the commands of Christ to love God, to love one another, and to make disciples (see Matt. 22:37–40; 28:18–20). Then, having stated that goal, the rancher will flesh it out in terms of behaviors and programs that are appropriate to the local situation, offering to be a modeler of ministry rather than the person who does the ministry single-handedly.

The rancher seeks out opportunities to empower others and applauds the expansion of caregiving. The desired objective is not less care but assured care.

Yes, pastors and staff are permitted to offer one-on-one care, but they will do so with the primary intent of equipping additional ministers—volunteers and staff members alike—to do the legitimate work of providing primary care and spiritual nurture to those in need, both within the church constituency and beyond.

When this goal becomes more important than the satisfaction of the minister, a church will be able to move beyond single-pastor ministry to multiple-pastor ministry and in so doing enlarge the flock.

Such is the kind of self-management of a leader that can make a most critical difference.

Self-Evaluation Moment

You and your family are on vacation, and you receive a message at your motel to phone somebody in the church whose name and number you do not recognize. As you receive this news, what is your attitude?

1. I knew I shouldn't go on vacation. They need me!

2. I wish my family could be a little more self-sacrificing. If we'd deny ourselves more, such as not being gone so long on this vacation, we'd have more time for ministry.

3. My family won't mind if we delay our outing so that I can return this call.

4. If it's a real emergency, I'm sure they'll contact this week's deacon on call, who will handle it just fine.

5. I can't believe the secretary or elders released our vacation phone number to anyone other than our key leadership! I'd better give them more training in not allowing themselves to be so dependent on me.

Comment: If interpreted from a care-centered motivation, the higher the number, the more you demonstrated rancher characteristics.

For Further Thought

1. The opening paragraph of this chapter contains this confession: "I ministered as if the world's salvation hung on my being available for everyone's primary-care needs." What Scriptures would support that perspective? What passages would challenge it?

2. What are some of your experiences in giving away ministry? How did you feel? How did people respond? What insights have you gained?

3. How do you feel about this statement: One way to distinguish the activities of paid, professional clergy is by the fact that the vast majority of their hours go to leadership development. What is the reasoning behind this view? What would be the most widespread objection to it?

4. Which self-evaluation moment in this chapter gave you the greatest insight about yourself? On a scale of one to ten, with one being the consummate sheepherder and ten being a full-scale rancher, where do you stand? Why?

8

What About "Problem People"?

How would the following business advice apply to your church? *When wooing prospects, always remember your shareholders. If you focus so heavily on servicing new prospects that you have no money left over to pay dividends, the stock owners will take away your privilege of researching new-customer interests.*

At issue is a principle called stakeholder symmetry, which any effective leader must understand, whether in the business world or the church.

This concept says that every organization includes a huge contingent of people called stakeholders—those with an investment in what you are doing. They care very deeply that in your enthusiastic pursuit of the organization's future you do not forget the powerful contingent who helped create the past.

If, in reaching for what could be, you allow the balance scales to tip too far, you will lose the loyalty of those who treasure what has been.

Suppose you decide, for example, that your Sunday school could be replaced with a program better designed to meet the needs of the population segment your church is targeting. Suppose, further, that those now participating in your Sunday school oppose your plan. If you are not careful, you may find that while you row forward toward a preferred future, your Sunday school people will drop stones in your canoe.

Stakeholder symmetry offers this warning: While you paddle forward with the progressives, watch out that certain partisan groups do not sink you.

Almost every person, in every church, is party to a special interest. One crowd may have a deep concern about your church building, another about your Christian day school, another about foreign missions, and yet another about denominational issues.

As you lay plans for the future, you would be wise to take all your interest groups into account. Otherwise, any who feel left out or alienated may, as soon as they can find the opportunity, defeat your overall progress.

Who Are Your Stakeholders?

How do you identify your stakeholder groups? First, realize that some will be insiders, such as staff, choir, board, Sunday school people, youth, day-school leaders, and so forth. Others may be outsiders, such as neighbors in whose yards your members park, city officials who fear your vote, denominational officials hoping for a budgetary contribution, and the like. All these people hold an interest in the church you serve and its operation.

Also, do not overlook the invisible realm. It is fully appropriate to identify God both as owner and stakeholder in the progress of his church. After all, Scripture likens the church to the bride of Christ (Eph. 5:25–32; Rev. 22:17), the body of Christ (Rom. 12:4–8; 1 Cor. 12:12–27; Col. 1:18), the family of God (Gal. 6:10; Heb. 2:11; 1 Peter 4:17), and many other relationships of united purpose.

In opposition to God and his angels are the devil and other evil principalities. Their stake in your church is to thwart your advances.

Second, remember that stakeholders have the ability to make choices regarding the resources they control, whether tangible things like money, or interpersonal influences such as the ability to give or withhold permission. Their participation or boycott is based on their own agendas, purposes, and goals, which may or may not be in agreement with what you are trying to do.

Third, be aware of the significance of the relationship between one stakeholder and another. For example, a coalition may form between nongrowth-minded city officials and taxpayers whose homes neighbor the church properties. They may form a powerful network to oppose the expansion of the church's parking lot. In this case their vested interest affects the outcome of your organization's growth, even if it only is to resist your encroachment on their way of life.

A New Slant on Berry Buckets

If there is any one stakeholder issue that most frequently causes grief in churches, it stems from a combination of age and tenure factors. This problem, more than any other I have observed, is a major dynamic in pastoral dismissals and church splits. I summarize the principles of the problem by calling it the "berry bucket" theory of church leadership.[1]

The image is this. In the root cellar of my uncle's farm was a two-shelf storage space for berries gathered from his garden. He dated the berries, as they awaited further processing, by placing yesterday's pick on the bottom shelf and today's pick on the top.

Churches are like root cellars in the sense that they tend to store the "crop" in different identifiable clusters. On the bottom shelf is the older guard, and on the top shelf is the newer crowd.

The determining factor is the tenure of the present senior pastor. Those on the bottom shelf, who have been at the church longer than the pastor, are "formerberries." The "newberries," on the top shelf, are those drawn to the church since the present pastor's arrival.

One further distinction: Those *younger* than the pastor are either "*junior* formerberries" or "*junior* newberries." Those *older* than the pastor are "*senior* formerberries" or "*senior* newberries."

What help does this classification system offer? Each of these four groups has a different perception of the pastor's role. Each group, in turn, requires a different leadership style (see Figure 5).

By recognizing that there are basically four "buckets" represented in a typical church, a pastor can learn to perceive the dissimilar expectations each group brings. In so doing the pastor can anticipate and nip in the bud much church conflict.

Figure 5
The Berry Bucket Theory

Older Newcomers
(Senior Newberries)

- Suggest
- Show homework

Younger Newcomers
(Junior Newberries)

- Make appropriate suggestions
- Expect to be followed

See pastor as "leader" or commander

Polarization Potential

some follow pastor

some side with elders

See pastor as "chaplain" or hired hand

- Ask permission
- Provide leadership to their agenda

Older Longtermers
(Senior Formerberries)

- Bring reform without alienating other groups

Younger Longtermers
(Junior Formerberries)

© 1992 Carl F. George

Here is how each of these groups would view you if you were their senior pastor:

1. Junior newberries. The easiest people to lead are the junior newberries. They are younger than you and they came to the church after you. Therefore, they tend to take your word about life experiences (you're probably "ahead" of them) and about what happened earlier in the church (they weren't there, but you were). They almost have no choice but to be influenced by you.

Junior newberries perceive you as their leader or even as commanding officer. In most cases, all you need do for them to follow you is to announce where you are going and then to lead the charge.

A forty-two-year-old minister, for instance, will find that the people most excited about joining the church will be, in most cases, in the thirty-five to forty age range. In other words, most pastors find it easiest to win people two-to-ten years younger than themselves.

2. Senior newberries. Those parishioners who are older than their pastor may respect his or her judgment in some areas, but because they have "been around" longer, they withhold judgment on other issues.

For example, if I visit a church led by a younger clergyman, I can usually buy his enthusiasm for marriage and his excitement about his young family. When it comes to his advice on how to handle my teenage kids, however, I will hear him out but probably not accept it with full credibility.

My wife and I have six children, five of whom have already turned thirteen. As a result, I am quick to spot simplistic or unrealistic statements about parenting teens. A younger pastor has not experienced the life stages of people like me twenty years his senior.

How do pastors work with senior newberries? They suggest what they would like to see done, they present their rationale and research, and they invite their senior newberries to follow along.

Pastors cannot automatically expect to be trusted until they can show their homework. Why? Senior newberries have lived long enough to see leaders behave foolishly. They will not follow their pastor until they are convinced that he or she is acting with wisdom.

3. Senior formerberries. The hardest people to lead are those who were part of the church before you came and who are also older

than you. Although they may belong to the group that called you to lead their church, that is not what they really want you to do.

Rather, they probably think they hired you to stand in their pulpit, lead the worship service, preach, help them raise their budget, handle weddings and funerals, and visit them in the hospital. In short, they frequently view the pastor as the chaplain or the hired hand.

Senior formerberries cannot be led in the same way as junior newberries. You lead the younger group by suggestion and excitement—by a dream appropriate to you in your present life stage. They accept it, because they like you and can identify with your vision. But the group who preceded you had all kinds of ideas before you came. You represented only a part of their ideal for their future. You were the best fit they could find.

To provide leadership to senior formerberries, you need to listen carefully as you ask them, "What do you think God is calling this church to do and be? What direction are we heading? Where are we going? What are we doing?"

Then provide leadership for them to reach *their* objectives. As you empower their dreams, they will increasingly trust—and permit—your leadership to the rest of the church.

Or, to restate it humorously, the minister's modus operandi goes like this: I am their leader so I *follow* them. As soon as I find out where they want to go, I'll stand at the head of the line so I don't look bad.

I would add: Do not get too far ahead of that line or you will turn around and not find them. Instead, stay close enough that you can know when they turn, and then change course with them.

Young pastors often have a hard time with this perspective, because it may be alien to their dreams of exerting power. There is a difference between leading and providing leadership, however. Or, to repeat one unknown wit: The difference between a leader and a martyr is about three paces.

The longer you are in the church, the more trust you earn from senior formerberries, and the more the church's vision will unify around your personal vision.

Are there any exceptions? One involves founding pastors. In some ways no one can "outformerberry" them, because no one was there ahead of them. Church-planting pastors, therefore, frequently do not have to deal with as many permission issues as clergy in established churches.

Lyle Schaller points out another important exception. Some long-established mainline churches seem dead in the water. When you ask where they are going, the people indicate that what they are best at is sitting. Schaller says their primary agenda is to avoid getting very deeply involved. His advice to pastors is, "Don't try to outpassive the passive." In other words, try to stay connected with the church, keep loving them, but also set before them some goals consistent with what they are capable of accomplishing. In the process, teach them then to be more active.[2]

4. Junior formerberries. These are usually the children of the senior formerberries. They are the hardest group to peg, because sometimes they accept the view of their elders (the senior formerberries) and sometimes they side with newcomers to the church (the newberries).

Avoiding Forced Terminations and Schisms

Pastors soon discover that these four types of people are not led with equal ease. Each needs a different set of signals.

Pastors frequently observe the greatest polarization between only two of these groups: the senior formerberries and the junior newberries. These two "buckets" are usually the most distinct from each other in both identity and leadership needs.

Further, a minister who has been at a church for a while can easily develop quite a substantial following of newberries. In many cases, he or she will attract several newberries for each formerberry present. This circumstance often results in the pastor concentrating attention on the newer blood.

The usual next progression is that the pastor fails to give leadership to both groups. The older guard becomes more or less ignored. Leadership, by default, goes to the junior newberries. After all, they represent a sizeable percentage of the church and they are excited about both their minister and their church.

But in the process, who feels neglected and has their feelings hurt? Senior formerberries. Who, in turn, has the greatest ability to hurt the pastor? In most cases, senior formerberries.

This kind of strained relationship is often at the root of forced terminations and church splits. Senior formerberries tend to control most of the keys: to the church kitchen, to the church vehicles, to the treasury, and to the boardroom. That spells clout.

Pastors must think of themselves not as leaders of one big church family but as leaders of groups within the whole, who give attention to the persons who require it as appropriate to their level of need.

Far better, then, to learn how to employ different leadership styles. Doing so may involve wearing two, three, or four hats a day. With every berry bucket the pastor thinks, Which hat do I have on now? Am I the leader of the junior newberries? Am I providing leadership to the senior formerberries? Am I to show my homework to the junior formerberries, or what?

> Pastors must think of themselves not as leaders of one big church family but as leaders of groups within the whole, who give attention to the persons who require it as appropriate to their level of need.

Sometimes the minister becomes confused and cries out, "Who am I?" It may take time, but a skilled leader can learn how to keep these hats dusted off and to switch them appropriately.

Problem Opportunities from Your Own Background

As ministers ask, Who am I? and try to develop more effective leadership skills, they sometimes discover that one of their greatest obstacles is themselves—in particular, their own unresolved personal and family issues.

Recovery and development are a lifelong process. I myself am a product of a family marked by several generations of deep pain. The way I compensated for it followed the same path many Christians have taken: I became a workaholic.

I hide from my pain in endless work. I often put in seventy hours a week. When I cannot accomplish enough work during the daytime, I put my family to bed, get up in the middle of the night, and work some more. My wife says, and rightly so, that I would rather work than sleep.

I am a driven man. As a result, I have difficulty feeling like a worthy person if I am not putting in those kinds of hours.

I once set a target of working only sixty hours a week, as a first step of progress. But that took so much work that I became exhausted.

Through insights I gained from the twelve-step recovery movement and teachings about family dysfunction, I became aware that my workaholism caused serious repercussions.

I remember how I would come home at night after a fourteen-hour day of pastoring a several-hundred-person church and managing our church's equally large Christian school. I would unload my pockets onto the bedroom dresser and find a note about a death call at the hospital, or a critically ill patient, or something similar, and feel I had to deal with it personally.

Why did I think that working inordinate hours, pushing myself to the point of fatigue and sickness, was truly honoring to God? Whom was I trying to impress? What kind of fatherly and husbandly duties was I avoiding by working so much?

My recovery began the day I repented of this self-deception. I am now a recovering workaholic, with a long way to go. I have lost more battles than I have won, but at least I am not kidding myself anymore.

The principle, which can apply to any pastor or layperson, is this: A surprising amount of our struggle to be leaders comes from misguided notions about ourselves and our need to do ministry when, in fact, God would be far more pleased if we would see that ministry got done.

Sometimes the matter is merely one of well-intended but nonetheless nonstrategic priorities. For me it was an issue of lying to myself.

Ministry fatigue is not God's gift to church leaders. Rather, one of its sources can be traced to the consequence of self-deceit, with the result that we work harder instead of smarter. Anyone who takes this concept to heart will have made a major step toward revising his or her life and goals as a manager and leader.

God is willing to forgive me. But he also wants me to pursue an alternative route so I do not fall into the same trap again.

Take a Deacon Next Time

What could I have done when I unloaded my pockets and found that message about a hospital call? Why not phone one of our church's deacons? If he had agreed to accept the honor of being called a deacon, then I should call him, whether it seemed to be a convenient time or not.

The first time we would go together to the hospital. He would observe me, join with me in caring, and then debrief afterward. The next time he could go without me. Ideally, he would bring another deacon and train him. And I would see that they were both applauded as champions.

If, in working seventy hours a week, I always had an apprentice present, my overload would not have lasted long. Why? There would be so many apprentices who wanted to work that they would have gobbled up the primary-care ministry I was trying to do.

The Church Leader's Personal Life

What about other ministry frustrations and pressures that clergy and active lay leaders face? Could some of them likewise be rooted in dysfunctional habits? How many issues in the typical leader's personal life stem from unrecognized self-deception?

Take, for example, the motivation of saving face. How much leadership behavior is driven by a need to look good in front of others? How many ministers' wives, out of fear of being criticized for not supporting their husbands, never ask themselves, What do *I* want? Instead they behave codependently[3] toward their church, allowing the question, What does the congregation want? to control their every decision. How many pastoral couples are so dominated by a need to maintain a pretense that they cover up their times of need when things are not faring well with their marriage or children?

Suppose the pastor of your church has a wife and small children. Would there ever be a time when he could say the following without feeling guilty or projecting blame? "No, my wife is at home and probably won't be here Sunday, either. She's exhausted, and we've neglected our kids recently, and the way you guys ring the phone at the parsonage, her only chance for quiet family time is when you're here at the church building meeting with me."

Or, consider the idea of a church as an addictive organization. The book *The Subtle Power of Spiritual Abuse* relates the true account of the young pastor who says to his board, "I'm really hurting. Our family is not being spiritually fed, we're not surviving on our sustenance budget, we can't pay our bills, and the stress is unbelievable."

The chairman of the board responds, "Pastor, I rule you out of order; you're not on the agenda." This story shows a pastor who is finally willing to say, "Help!" The unfortunate response implies, "You can't get well. If you do, our sickness will show up, too. Therefore, that's not to be discussed here."[4]

In this story it seems that the scoundrel was the board member. Had I cited another true case study, which reversed the roles, the fault could seem to rest with the pastor. In reality, no person is the real culprit. The villain is a system, and everyone in it can become victim to it.

More Are Addicts Than Acknowledge It

We could examine any number of topics, from adrenaline addiction to resentment in the parsonage or the home of an active layperson. The relevant lesson from the recovery community is that the problems seen in the drunk are not confined to people who abuse alcohol. Our bodies create excitements that behave like alcohol in that they preoccupy us and drive our feelings. The net result is that many more of us are addicted than go around wearing the badge.

Self-Evaluation Moment

1. How do you feel about the idea that many church leaders are motivated, in part, by unaddressed codependencies?

2. If you had to peg one potential codependency in your life, what would it be? How serious an influence is that addictive behavior on your ministry? on your family?

I find in my work with churches that the first thing to collapse on the road to addiction is people's clear view of themselves. It is almost as if they look in the mirror and see not themselves but a picture of a perfected self, one free from all addiction. With this loss of perspective the progression can continue until they become blind even to the feedback of those who are in a position to tell them, especially their intimates. Finally they lose their ability to balance work and home life.

As alienation grows within their families, their flight from intimacy creates two hideous consequences. First, they lose their spirituality, the ability to feel toward God and to respond to the pricks of conscience. The insides of their souls feel flatlined. No quickening at the mention of the name of God. No looking forward to a time of solitude in prayer. Pursued by the hound of heaven, they race onward in their frantic business. They hope that somehow God will catch up with them. At the same time, they are terrified to allow him to come close.

> Addicts hope that somehow God will catch up with them. At the same time, they are terrified to allow him to come close.

Second, they can lose their personal morality. "But how can I lose my personal morality," asks the Christian who has the addiction, "if I'm faithful to my spouse? I couldn't even be accused of flirting!" The sleeping around that catches so much press attention is often a suicidal cry. It traces back to desperate pastors who have lost their way and decided to end it all. They cannot build up the nerve to drive off a cliff, so they take a secretary to a motel and symbolically do the same thing.

Addicts lose their personal morality by two lies. First is the falsehood of denial when they assert, "I don't have a problem." Then, more insidiously, they lie to protect their supply of addictive substance. Pornographic addicts stash their girlie magazines, alcoholics cover up their whiskey cache, and church leaders, if they are workaholics, protect their supply of work. To them, work is righteous, work is right, work is what God expects, work is an escape from the evils of humanity, work is a deliverer.

Are workaholics not too busy working to have time to create lies? How do they protect the supply of addictive substance? With a little voice that whispers, as they unpack their pockets and find a reminder of an unfinished need, "The sacrifice will be worth it, because this is what God called me to do."

That response, for the workaholic, is a lie if he or she thinks, It's okay to neglect my family; or, No one else can do the job as well; or, Only I am willing to make the necessary sacrifices to meet this need.

For a while spouses or children may protest. In most cases, though, they gradually surrender and behave codependently themselves. "Well, if it's the work of God, then I guess we'll have to help you do it." They learn that survival means cooperating with the family lie.

Whether or not the family cooperates, the workaholic is unavailable to them emotionally because of preoccupation with work. As a result, the family members, constantly reaching for approval and emotional security, develop self-image problems. The hole in their souls leads them to a lifestyle of wanting to help too much. That quest may fulfill itself in their choosing codependent spouses or codependent careers. Their messianic drive says, "I, and only I, can make a difference in all of those people's lives."

The person who feels the greatest trap is usually the pastoral spouse, especially if that person is a woman who devotes great energy to support her husband's ministry. This clergy spouse often has enormous feelings of both inadequacy and anger. Worse, she feels a second damnation, because she decides that her emotions are unspiritual, an outlook which only adds to her despondency. She has given up her heart and life, her body and mind, and now finds herself unable to complain through her pain.

Grabbing On to Hope

The time has come when many people are blowing the whistle. From Christian psychologists to veteran pastors, a rally cry is going out: "Now that we've finally defined workaholism and other forms of addiction and codependency as a mismanagement of ministry, let's not tolerate it one minute longer."

What is recovery about? Its theological roots grow in the rich soil of God's grace. God reconciles us to himself and renews us day by day, not by our good works but by his riches in Christ Jesus (2 Cor. 5:17–21; Eph. 2:4–10; Phil. 4:12–13).

That grace creates the solid living hope described in many Scripture passages, such as 1 Peter 1:3–9, and affirmed in this prayer of the ancient church: "Although man lost the friendship of God through sin, God has offered covenants to man, and God's prophets have taught mankind to hope for salvation."[5]

We addicts have hope, because God gives us a salvation: not only life with him in heaven but deliverance for here and now as we are freed from our addictive lies. Repentance of sin truly leads to wholeness.

Read these twelve steps of Alcoholics Anonymous (with only slight modification for Christian purposes as noted by the brackets), which offer a liturgy for dealing with sin:

1. We admitted we were powerless over (name the [sin])—that our lives had become unmanageable.
2. We came to believe that a power [Jesus Christ], greater than ourselves, could restore us to sanity.
3. We made a decision to turn our will and our lives over to the care of God, as we understood him.
4. We made a searching and fearless moral inventory of ourselves.
5. We admitted to God, to ourselves, and to another human being the exact nature of our wrongs.
6. We are entirely ready to have God remove all these defects of character.
7. We humbly ask him to remove our shortcomings.
8. We have made a list of all persons we have harmed, and became willing to make amends to them all.
9. We will make direct amends to such people whenever possible, except when to do so would injure them or others.
10. We continue to take personal inventory, and when we are wrong promptly admit it.
11. We sought through prayer and meditation to improve our conscious contact with God as we understood him, praying

only for the knowledge of his will for us and the power to carry that out.

12. And, having had a spiritual awakening as a result of these steps, we try to carry this message to [those Jesus brings our way], and to practice these principles in all our affairs.[6]

This list is a life preserver for people drowning in a storm. It is for people desperately trying to find the love, grace, and companionship of God. Even though many Christians, including myself, have serious reservations about some of the things taught by the twelve-step movement, this more than any other approach I know helps addicts deal forthrightly with their sin.

Availing oneself of group support is a critical component, because most of us do not have either the clarity of sight on ourselves or the developed disciplines to follow through on the process of recovery. Most of us need to come alongside other sympathetic people who will say, "You're not slipping back into those old patterns, are you?" or "It appears that you're falling into those old patterns. What are you going to do so that you won't have more to confess next week than you do this week?"

In the twelve-step community, the people who have made the most progress have done so through sponsorship. Someone was willing to be intimately involved in their process of recovery and say, when needed, "Cut the self-deception. You are slipping and you know it. I can smell it, you can feel it, and anybody who is close to you knows it. Now stop it. What is driving you to do this? Let's deal with it!"

How many times someone falls off the wagon is immaterial. Jesus said to Peter, "Simon, you're going to betray me." Simon answered, "No, not me, Lord." "Yes, you will betray me. I'm praying for you that after you have recovered, you will strengthen your brethren" (paraphrase of Luke 22:31–34).

Listening to God

What do Christian addicts need to hear? I believe God wants to say, "My daughter or son, I have everything under control. Sit in my lap a little longer, because after you leave me, what's going to happen next will endure only if it's in line with what I'm doing. Everything else will perish. More than fill your mind with information or drive your body to accomplish programs, you need to learn to live in my love. Abide in me."

Would such a perspective encourage people to give less of themselves to the Lord's work? Would it hamper someone's obeying Jesus' command to "take up his cross daily and follow me" (Luke 9:23)? No; it would achieve just the opposite. The wholeness I describe will motivate people to serve God as Jesus did—not with anger but with joy (John 15:11; Heb. 12:2), and not with a drive to be accepted but with good works motivated by God's tremendous grace (Eph. 2:8–10).

I see the day coming when the Western church will be known as the place that offers health. Church leaders will know how to give permission for people to develop relational ministry, and the caring, nurturing groups of strugglers who have found bread in the presence of Jesus Christ will invite others to their table. Forgiveness, healing, and deliverance from addictive sin will be multiplied across the face of this continent.

Let us leaders set the pace by personally participating in such a community, be willing to let down the barriers, and speak with candor of our own human and spiritual needs. Let us forge ahead and create such communities where they do not now exist.

Let us hasten the day when this new order will come, as God grants each of us the freedom to stop the lie and become whole. Not somehow, but triumphantly![7]

I see the day coming when the Western church
will be known as the place that offers health.

For Further Thought

1. Do you agree with the berry bucket concept of a church's composition and of the leader wearing different hats when working with different groups? Why or why not?

2. Who are the main stakeholder groups within your church? outside your church?

3. In what ways is stakeholder symmetry at work among your parishioners? Who are the chief senior formerberries? the chief junior newberries? If there is friction between these groups at present, what does church leadership need to do to help them work together?

4. How many pastors or heavily involved laypeople do you know who struggle with workaholism? Of the person you know who is the most recovered, what pathway did God use?

5. What message would God say to you about your own addictive behaviors? If he were to use a Scripture text, which would he emphasize to you?

PART 3

Break Specific
Growth Barriers

9

How to Break the 200 Barrier

This chapter begins with a number of assumptions. It counts on your church's leadership having both a vision for growth and a commitment to it.[1] It supposes that you do *not* want to communicate to your visitors that you love your present size and want to remain that way. It presumes that your church knows how to attract newcomers and thus draws a flow (or trickle) of first-time guests.[2] It assumes that you are willing to modify your leadership style in ways that encourage growth, such as to make the shift from sheepherder to rancher.

In addition, this chapter trusts that at the heart of your mission is the life-changing good news that Jesus Christ came to seek and to save the lost (Luke 19:10).

In short, I am writing to people who are experiencing personal spiritual renewal, whose churches are beginning to reap a harvest, and who want additional resources and advice for making the most of their ministry potential.

Your New Peer Group

Through hundreds of consultations and thousands of pastoral surveys we have learned something very significant: Churches have more in common by their size than by their denomination, tradition, location, age, or any other single, isolatable factor.[3]

Figure 6
America's Weekly Worship Attendance
Based on a Survey of 115,374 Churches
in 9 Denominations (Total of all services, adults and children)

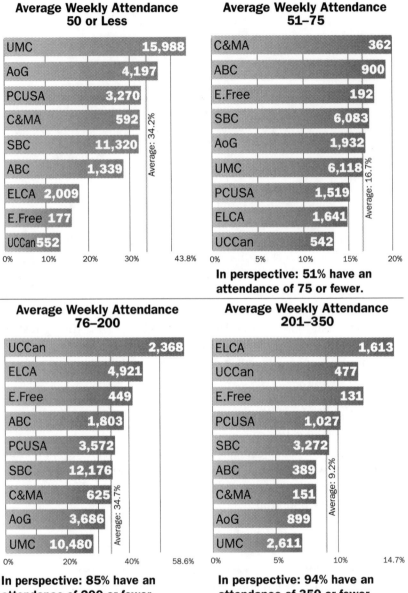

Average Weekly Attendance 50 or Less

UMC	15,988
AoG	4,197
PCUSA	3,270
C&MA	592
SBC	11,320
ABC	1,339
ELCA	2,009
E.Free	177
UCCan	552

Average: 34.2%

0%   10%   20%   30%   43.8%

Average Weekly Attendance 51–75

C&MA	362
ABC	900
E.Free	192
SBC	6,083
AoG	1,932
UMC	6,118
PCUSA	1,519
ELCA	1,641
UCCan	542

Average: 16.7%

0%   5%   10%   15%   20%

In perspective: 51% have an attendance of 75 or fewer.

Average Weekly Attendance 76–200

UCCan	2,368
ELCA	4,921
E.Free	449
ABC	1,803
PCUSA	3,572
SBC	12,176
C&MA	625
AoG	3,686
UMC	10,480

Average: 34.7%

0%   20%   40%   58.6%

In perspective: 85% have an attendance of 200 or fewer.

Average Weekly Attendance 201–350

ELCA	1,613
UCCan	477
E.Free	131
PCUSA	1,027
SBC	3,272
ABC	389
C&MA	151
AoG	899
UMC	2,611

Average: 9.2%

0%   5%   10%   14.7%

In perspective: 94% have an attendance of 350 or fewer.

Notes
1. Summary statements are based on the number of churches, not the number of denominations.
2. Source: Annual reports from each denominational office.

Average Weekly Attendance
351–500

E.Free	65
ELCA	486
PCUSA	300
SBC	1,039
ABC	124
C&MA	48
AoG	293
UMC	794
UCCan	86

Average: 2.8%

0%   2%   4%   6.1%

In perspective: 97.6% have an attendance of 500 or fewer.

Average Weekly Attendance
501–800

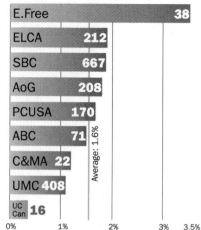

E.Free	38
ELCA	212
SBC	667
AoG	208
PCUSA	170
ABC	71
C&MA	22
UMC	408
UCCan	16

Average: 1.6%

0%   1%   2%   3%   3.5%

In perspective: 99.2% have an attendance of 800 or fewer

Average Weekly Attendance
801–1,000

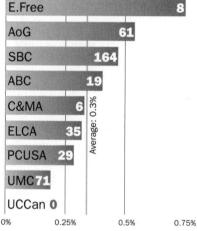

E.Free	8
AoG	61
SBC	164
ABC	19
C&MA	6
ELCA	35
PCUSA	29
UMC	71
UCCan	0

Average: 0.3%

0%   0.25%   0.5%   0.75%

In perspective: 99.5% have an attendance of 1,000 or fewer.

Average Weekly Attendance
1,001 or more

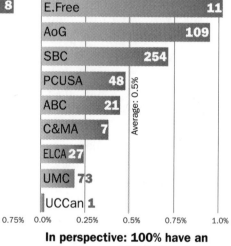

E.Free	11
AoG	109
SBC	254
PCUSA	48
ABC	21
C&MA	7
ELCA	27
UMC	73
UCCan	1

Average: 0.5%

0.0%   0.25%   0.5%   0.75%   1.0%

In perspective: 100% have an attendance of 20,000 or fewer.

Key
(denomination, number of churches, year of data)

ABC=	American Baptist	4,666 (1991 data)	PCUSA= Presbyterian	9,935 (1990 data)
AoG=	Assemblies of God	11,385 (1991 data)	SBC= Southern Baptist	34,975 (1991 data)
C&MA=	Christian & Miss. Alliance	1,813 (1991 data)	UCCan= United Church of Canada	4,042 (1991 data)
E. Free=	Evangelical Free	1,701 (1990 data)	UMC= United Methodist	35,540 (1991 data)
ELCA=	Lutheran	10,947 (1991 data)		

©1992 Carl F. George

In other words, leaders ministering in a church with a worship attendance (adults and children)[4] of 200 will develop a sense of camaraderie far more quickly and naturally with leaders from another church of the same size, even if from a different denomination or tradition, than they will with colleagues from their communion who represent a church of 50 or 75.

The typical church in North America is small. Half of this continent's approximately 400,000[5] churches run about 75 in weekly attendance.[6]

When your church breaks through 100 in its regular attendance, you as a pastor or key lay leader will begin to ask yourself, Am I wrong to have started to see things differently from most of my ministry colleagues?

The answer is no. In trying to find some wisdom appropriate to your next step of growth, you are discovering that your peers, for the most part, have not had to deal with the questions and issues you are now facing.

At the 100 mark, your church has become larger than 60 percent of your peers'; at 140, 75 percent; at 200, 85 percent; at 350, 93 percent; and by 500, 95 percent. When your average attendance climbs beyond 1,000 (99th percentile), your identity is so distinct that this chapter could list every such North American church by name.[7] At about 3,300 you enter the ranks of the "100 Largest Churches" in North America. (See also Figure 6).[8]

Most available resources are geared, predictably, to the 85 percent of churches that have not yet broken the 200 barrier and overlook the special needs of the growing and larger church.

This chapter summarizes certain key issues necessary to break the 200 barrier. This figure is not an exact or magical number (the range is actually between 50 and 350), but it does represent a critical growth limiter that the vast majority of churches hit.

The next chapter will focus on the 400 barrier, which represents a second decisive growth point in the 350-to-600-person attendance level. Chapter 11 touches on the key issues necessary to break the 800 barrier, a plateau most churches hit between 600 and 1,200.

Finally, chapter 12 discusses what may be referred to as the 10,000-down-to-10 barrier. It describes how to grow bigger by becoming smaller. For that reason I have entitled the chapter, "How to Break the *Care* Barrier."

Prewire the Crisis

When I checked into the hospital for surgery several years ago, the nurse stuck an intravenous needle in my arm. "What's that for?" I asked her.

"It's a precaution. If an emergency happens, we'll be ready," she said.

What a powerful analogy of how churches can better administer care in Jesus' name! We can "prewire" people so that when a crisis occurs, the church can spring into action. We hope our people will not have to face medical tragedy, emotional grief, loneliness, conflict, and other forms of need. But since they do, why not prepare for it?

This chapter reviews how the rancher style of leadership, as presented in chapters 1, 6, and 7, makes the necessary preparations to handle people's needs. As a result, the church that has put the interpersonal relationships and supportive organizational system in place before the crisis occurs is able to offer enough care that it can break one growth barrier after another.

Here, then, is a summary of what is necessary to break early growth barriers from the 75 barrier through the 200 barrier.

1. Exude a contagious desire to grow. This motivational factor makes a critical difference. If you lack a compelling vision or holy imagination for what God wants to do through you and through your church, review the implications of chapters 2 and 3.

2. Clearly articulate why, humanly speaking, your church has grown and what active ingredients need to be continued and stoked. Chapters 4 and 5 were designed to help you diagnose your church's historic track record.

3. Determine what steps are next for you to shift from sheepherder to rancher, and vigorously pursue them. Have you analyzed your ministry style and personal behavior patterns and identified one or two specific improvements to make? How will you know, two weeks from now, whether you have grown in these areas? For guidance, review chapters 6 and 7.

4. Deal with institutional factors that can keep a church under 200. Why do your senior formerberries, as defined in chapter 8, not always receive newcomers with open arms? Your present membership probably has a strong desire to preserve its social intimacy. Their present size allows everyone to know, or to know about, everyone else. As a result, they are probably fearful of anything—such as new people—that threatens the closeness and familiarity they have with one another.

People, including Christians, like to be comfortable. If they are convinced that growth will upset the family feeling they associate with "their" church, they may establish a surprising number of turf-protection barricades to keep new members from being absorbed.

5. Guard against a small-church mentality creeping back in. If you, like most ministers and lay leaders, have been shaped by a long-term pattern of small-church thinking, be prepared for the pressures that may lure you back into that paradigm.

One source will be the expectations of your church people, perhaps even of your spouse, and also your codependent tendency to be controlled by them. These dynamics, which range from uninformed lifelong habits to downright sabotage, receive attention in chapter 8.

Another pressure to return to the old will be the disequilibrium you experience as you make the transition to a new peer group who are asking the same kinds of questions you are. That awkwardness was described in the section of chapter 2 on vision limiters and reintroduced at the beginning of this chapter.

Perhaps the most subtle appeal to a life of flock petting, with its accompanying cap on growth, may come during a burst of apparently prosperous ministry. Suppose, for example, you develop your ranching skills and release a number of your people to function as lay shepherds. Suppose, further, that through the ministry of one of those whom you are discipling, a well-connected family in your community experiences a spiritual rebirth and becomes involved in your church. They, in turn, draw four other households to the church. These four newcomers likewise invite their friends, and a growth momentum is born.

Your temptation, as you observe these junior newberries trying to assimilate into the existing networks and structures of the church, might be to pop on your sheepherder cap and each time you notice a relationship gap become the primary care giver.

Or, consider the true case of a couple who had an ideal situation for becoming the consummate sheepherders. He, the sole pastor of this church, could prepare an excellent sermon in ten hours a week. Then he would put in sixty additional hours of hands-on need meeting. She, though not officially on staff, volunteered more hours than many full-time ministers put in. Their married children lived out of state, and they both seemed to have the gift of "perpetual hospitality" at their home, which adjoined the church property.

A person could walk into the church building during daylight hours, seven days a week, and anticipate being greeted by this pastor or his wife. In the evening, neither seemed too busy to take a call at home.

These wonderful Christian people went to heroic efforts to see to it that they were always available. As a result, they helped build the church to an attendance of 700.

Unfortunately, however, they collapsed. He had a coronary arrest, and she became very resentful of how she felt the church had "done her husband in." They resigned and moved elsewhere, broken and discouraged.

My point? Even if sheepherding helps produce growth and carries you beyond the 200 barrier, you will reach a stopping point sooner or later. When you reach that capacity level, you will discover that your own health is in need of repair, both physically, emotionally, and probably spiritually. And your church members, whom you might have trained to expect omnipresent hand-holding from their minister, may hound you until you or your successor resumes that level of ministry.

6. Establish a network of lay-led small groups as the context for lay leadership development. Peter Wagner, one of today's leading authorities on church growth, says, "The major difference between the church under the 200 barrier and one over the 200 barrier is fellowship groups."[9] He explains why a church must move from single cell to multiple cell if it is to grow beyond 200:

> The group dynamic theory that underlies this is the rule of 40. Forty people is the ideal size for everyone to maintain face-to-face rela-

tionship with everyone else. In a church setting the group can expand to 80 and sustain most of the interpersonal qualities. However, when it goes past 80 toward 200, the relationships are increasingly strained. By the time it gets to 150 most groups are so stressed out that they can no longer handle the thought of strangers entering the group and thereby increasing the stress. Without knowing they are doing it or without even wanting to, they relate to strangers like two identical poles of magnets.[10]

As veteran church observer Elmer Towns confirms, the wave of the future is in body life through cell groups. "To be a whole church, it must have the *cell* as well as the *celebration*,"[11] he says. He finds this model to be eminently biblical:

> The large group in the Jerusalem church met for celebration, preaching, motivation and testimony (see Acts 3:11); and in small cells for fellowship, accountability, instruction and identity (see Acts 5:42). From these observations, I conclude that the norm for the New Testament church included both small cell groups and larger celebration groups.[12]

Imagine the potential as increasing numbers of laypeople are released to be coministers of care and nurture. Meeting in groups of approximately ten people—the time-tested, scientifically validated size that allows for optimal communication[13]—warehouses of underutilized Christians will prompt each other to love and good works.

Their challenge and ongoing encouragement will come from peers who know one another's spiritual gifts and who care enough that they will not allow a friend to settle into spectatorism. Because of the intimate, accountability-inviting context of an affinity-based group, participants will readily accept the call of God that accompanies the discovery of their gifts. The immediacy of the evangelism and discipleship that occurs in the lives of fellow cell members cannot help but shatter passivity. (Chapter 12 will present more insight into a systemic approach to lay-led small groups.)

For now, let me pose a question: If each of the world's largest churches (fellowships of 30,000 or more are found on every continent except North America) has found that a cell system is vital to its health and ongoing growth, then what is the implication for the vitality of *your* church as a potential church of 30,000?

My conclusion is this: Sooner or later, a constantly rekindled vision of open cells led by prayerful people replicating themselves through apprentice leaders is going to produce life-changing results—two-to-four converts per year per group. As staff members place priority on the cultivation of the lay leadership necessary to make this happen, the dynamics of cell fertility will inevitably take over, and much fruit will be harvested, including that of numerical church growth.

The implication? Make sure your people are lodged in a cell system where a lay pastoral team receives ongoing supervision and coaching from the professional staff of the church. See to it that the pastoral staff is infected with a vision so radical that it is tantamount, for many, to a change in profession: getting out of the ministry business and into a new assignment of making ministers.

Properties and Facilities

As a church grows toward and beyond the 200 barrier, the leadership frequently faces new questions about building programs, facility enlargements, and property acquisitions. Here are the questions I am asked most frequently. I will deal with multiple worship services in chapter 11.

1. Our people are talking about enlarging our facility to reduce overcrowding. *How do I know if that is the solution needed?*

Your most crucial capacity determiner stems from your parking availability, not your seating capacity (see example in Figure 7). In growing churches, lack of on-site parking often creates tension for both members and visitors. The rare exceptions are those located adjacent to public parking areas or to curbside parking on sidewalk-lined streets.

If you pastor a growing church that fills its auditorium on average to more than 80 percent of its capacity, then the overcrowdedness (over a two-to-three-year period) will tend to limit the growth of your church. Exceptions occur if you are ministering in an ethnic community that is underserved, if you have a strong cell system,

Figure 7
Site Loads for Multiple Services

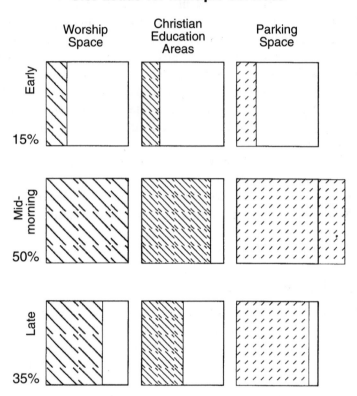

Parking, more than seating, often determines attendance capacity.

and/or if your church has an exceptional platform appeal such as miracle ministries, widely known and advertised musical talent, or regionally broadcast television or radio programming.

But do not be hasty in concluding that the 80 percent fill is your problem when, in reality, the barrier may be elsewhere. Divide your average attendance by two-and-a-half people per car. If you draw a lot of single adults, divide by one-and-a-half people per car. Do you have enough easy-to-reach parking spots?

Even if the answer is yes, you still might not be ready for a building program. Instead, a wise next step is to consider establishing dual usage of your current facilities.

If you are short on Sunday school space, install two Sunday school sessions, one before and one after the worship. If your auditorium is small, then offer two worship services with Sunday school in between. If you are tight all the way around, think about holding Sunday school and worship simultaneously. Send everybody from the first hour home and then repeat the process for the second hour. By creatively using your existing space without enlargement, you can increase your membership by 50 percent or better.

In short, if a church is serious about growth, it will demonstrate that commitment by making an adequate amount of parking available and by maximizing the use of its physical plant. The difference between pastors who can lead their churches forward and those who cannot frequently expresses itself over this issue: whether the pastor is willing to envision new facilities, raise the necessary money, and lead the parishioners through the accompanying pains of acquisition and adjustment.

If you can lead your people to accept the idea of a different use of their time and space, then you have probably developed the trust and skill necessary to lead them to do other things they need for growth overall.

2. Our church is almost ready for a building program. *Should we expand where we are or relocate?*

In theory it is easier to relocate than to expand, because land can be cheaper, building from scratch is easier than remodeling, and parking is choosable and plannable. In reality, however, most churches end up enlarging in their present locations.

I recommend you plan for both, remembering all the while that most of your solutions will not come together overnight.

First, establish a "green-line district" around your present church facility. This represents properties you would like to acquire. Begin buying them. Be careful, though, not to take on more debt than you can handle.

Over ten years, you can accumulate a sizeable amount of contiguous real estate. After the land has been unoccupied and out of tax service, the city fathers will be eager for you to put the land to better use.

Develop a plan for local expansion, and begin securing the necessary legal permissions. You will probably have to outlast certain local politicians, extremist environmental groups, and others with an antidevelopment attitude. Of course, if you decide that you own more real estate than you need, or if you opt to relocate, you can usually sell.

Meanwhile, make sure you are aware of every available option. Consider church planting and multicampus approaches. Have multiple worship services to maximize use of your present facilities.

If you think creatively and plan long range, you will ultimately develop the kind of campus you need.

3. Our church is looking for land. *Is there an optimal ratio of acreage to congregation size?*

One acre can handle between 100 and 300 people, depending on your programming, how many people drive to your services, the average number of people per car, and the "green space" requirements of your local zoning board.

Do not count on a traditional program to stack people in at 300 per acre. You will need several turns of the auditorium for that: maybe a Saturday-night service, back-to-back Sunday-morning services, and more home-based cell groups than on-premises Sunday school classes.

4. *What do you recommend for our church's property search?* We're choosing between a visible site that has an inadequate roadway and a hard-to-see location with easy access.

Accessibility is almost always more important than visibility. You may have a worship center perched on top of a hill, but if there is only one road leading up there, and it is not clearly marked, you are in trouble. The same principle holds for the church facility adjacent to a well-traveled highway but four confusing miles away from the exit ramp.

The more visible site inevitably costs more. You are better off to move in the direction of accessibility and use the dollars saved to advertise your church and its programs.

5. What are some common snags to watch for when we work with architects and city councils?

They are not always accurate in understanding your site-load needs. City codes, for example, may permit you to build an auditorium based on five or six seats per car in your parking lot. But church trends are for fewer and fewer people per car, especially in upper-middle-class and suburban situations. So your architect may fix you up legally, but you will encounter the immediate problem of not being able to park everyone.

Instead, make your own site-load calculation by tallying the total number of bodies on a per-hour basis. That is, take your busiest hour—say Sunday at 11:00 A.M.—and calculate the anticipated capacity of your worship space including choir, plus your nursery, plus the number of people using your Christian education space (children and adults).

Next figure out how many people come per car during that busiest hour. Divide that number into your per-hour total and you have a more realistic site load (review Figure 7).

Be prepared, however, for the findings from your studies to lead you to make better use of your space. You will discover, for example, that if you emphasize home groups over traditional Sunday school, you will reduce parking needs on Sundays (not to mention the larger benefit of engendering greater care). Switching your youth group to the first hour on Sundays, or using three different choirs instead of one stay-all-morning choir, may likewise realign your parking area's pressure points.

6. I'm convinced that our community views our church as too crowded for anyone new, but our board doesn't feel that way. What should I do?

Unchurched people view churches in the same way legendary baseball player Yogi Berra described an overcrowded restaurant: "Don't go there to eat; nobody goes there, because you can never find a seat." In other words, "They're so successful that it's not worth going!" It takes only two seasons to teach an entire community that you do not have room for prospective new members. Even a 5 percent turn-away factor communicates that you are too full. Then the gripe factor comes into play: A satisfied customer tells three people, and a dissatisfied customer tells seven.

What to do? First, ask yourself if you have built a climate on your church board that genuinely wants growth. Or, would board members rather preserve their memory of the past? Do they see the grassy spot in front of the church building as the former swamp which they filled and cultivated, or as the next site for "phase two" of the parking lot plan?

Second, probe to find out if they are aware of how visitors feel. If your old-timers arrive early enough that they can park in the best spots, do they know that the newcomers must walk across icy slush or broken pavement?

In short, create a contagious vision of the harvest God wants to grant to your church.

7. In light of rising costs for land and buildings, we want to lease. What are the minimum facility requirements we should consider?

First, find major meeting space for worship. Often, this same area can accommodate large-group fellowship occasions as well. Ideally it will also be available during the week for times of leadership training.

In addition, you will want child-care space to accompany your big meetings. It should be clean, child safe, and easily accessible from your major meeting room(s).

Finally, you will need administration space for pastors and office help, and storage space for church equipment and supplies.

How does this list differ from that for a church building committee? The missing ingredient is classrooms. Historically, a huge percentage of a construction budget gets sunk into facilities, such as for teaching space, which are used only once a week. Churches of the future, particularly urban churches, will be pressured by economics to make greater use of home-based groups.

For Further Thought

1. How comfortable are you with the assumptions outlined at the beginning of this chapter?

2. What surprised you about the growth statistics cited in this chapter? What suspicions did you already have? Does your denomination or fellowship fit the norm?

3. Look over the summary of the issues necessary for breaking the 200 barrier. Which reflect a strength of your church? Which pinpoint areas of needed improvement?

4. How essential is the small group to the overall health of a church? to its numerical growth? Why?

5. What property and facilities issue is most pressing for your church? What are your top three options at present?

10

How to Break
the 400 Barrier

As a church moves beyond the 200 barrier it encounters a fresh
set of challenges. Certain issues that previously were of minor concern now take center stage. Pastors and lay leaders begin to ask new
questions about church boards, staffing, and delegation of duties.
These three administrative issues are pivotal if a church is to offer
adequate care to more than four hundred active participants.

What answers will your church give to the crucial questions this
raises? Your response will have a major influence on how quickly
and painlessly you are able to break the 400 barrier.

This chapter will not tell you where to find enough new people
that your attendance can reach four hundred. It assumes that your
current membership has an adequate contact base to serve far more
than four hundred newcomers. Rather, this chapter describes how to
prepare for, lead, and care for additional growth.

How Best to Work with Your Board

As a church moves beyond the two-hundred-person level and
begins to envision itself at the eight-hundred-person size, it must
make certain organizational shifts to continue in the growth process.
One of the most important issues to negotiate is the changing role of
the church governing board. Planning and administration must

become a staff function, not a board responsibility. That transition usually needs to be in motion to break through the 400 barrier.

When a church is small, its perceptions of executive officer, board, and ministry are tightly linked together. To most small-church eyes the tasks of these three cannot be differentiated.

At the smaller stage, the patriarchs, matriarchs, and heavy donors run the church, whether or not they are on the board. The real votes almost never take place in the board meetings. Instead, the decisions that determine whether the big donors and people of influence will back something are made in living rooms, on the phone, or over coffee. The board simply plays catch-up with what has been decided. The real power is based in an informal group, not in the pastor or board.

As a church increases in size, the oligarchy of power tends to be centered in the one or two closest friends of the senior pastor (or of the senior pastor's spouse), plus the pastor's closest aides on the staff. This group, typically fewer than a dozen people, exercises most of the control over the church.

If such a coterie is right with God, orthodox in doctrine, and balanced in its view of the church's mission, the church will accomplish great things. The board in this case merely documents and approves what has already been decided.

When a church reaches an average attendance of four hundred or so, generally the members of the board are the people who *can* make a difference or are the *spouses* of the people who can make a difference. The formal and informal power structures have come together. These boards are "dangerous," because they can actually accomplish something.

Boards Are Essential

At the same time, boards are essential for this stage of growth. The pastor who tries to lead a church without a board or to play games with it will soon encounter great trouble. The households represented on the board are typically of the primary donors, the primary influencers, the primary recruiters of volunteer energies, and even the primary conduits for reaching large segments of unchurched people.

The need for shared vision and camaraderie at the board level is so critical that it cannot be left to chance. An enthusiastic "Glad to see you! How 'ya been doing?" makes a huge difference in building an esprit de corps, as do pats on the back, good-natured ribbing, and other gestures of personal concern.

As the church enlarges beyond an attendance of four hundred, it becomes crucial to identify what roles are played by certain groups: (1) the chief executive officer and staff, (2) the board, (3) and the ministry leaders. Based on this analysis, certain shifts must occur to prepare for continued growth.

The team that must drive the program, provide the vision, do the planning, and create the budgets is the church staff, not the board. The term *staff* refers to people in management roles in a church's organization, regardless of whether they are paid or volunteer, ordained or lay, full-time or part-time, as long as they meet this qualification: They have agreed to take assignments from the senior leadership and be held accountable.

This staff then goes to the board mainly for approvals and policy. The board, as well as the other people of influence, comes to understand that the staff will provide direction, the board will provide policy, and everyone else—95 percent or more of the church—will be involved in hands-on ministry.

Dangers of a Small-Church Mentality

Most pastors and board members cut their ecclesiastical eyeteeth in a small church. A few may have gained experience in a medium-sized church, but it probably behaved like a small church. In either of those contexts the boards typically hire staff to do the ministry.

So, when the church is smaller, board members see themselves as the structurally empowered leaders of the church. They want to set the budget, the plan, and the dream. Then they want the paid, professional clergy to carry it out.

In other words, board members designate themselves as the managers and the church staff as the ministers (see Figure 8). That leaves the majority of the church in a spectatorish, inactive role at worst, and a semipassive dependency at best. This pattern helps

Figure 8

**Traditional Smaller Church
Expectations and Structures**

© 1992 Carl F. George

explain why so many North American churches do not grow (a perspective I will expand in chapter 12).

If a church is to become bigger, the staff must commission ministry and take policy direction from boards. That represents a world of difference from the typical small-church arrangement. This new set of roles requires an important transfer in the focus of initiative taking. Staff members pick up management responsibilities and keep their hands off the direct primary-care shepherding, except when they train laypeople for such ministry.

This new assignment causes dismay for many staff people who may feel the loss so deeply that they seek out a smaller church or a church with a smaller vision that will allow them a continued shepherding role. Or they feel that they do not want to handle the level of heat associated with the change. Many such staff people are too dependent on others to give them leadership to want that amount of accountability and responsibility to be laid on themselves. As a consequence, they bail out and go to places where someone else will take care of them.

Resistance to New Board Roles

Lay leaders likewise may buck the change from their setting the church's course to being a policy-making board. Certain laypersons derive a feeling of power from being able to say, "No, no, no" at the board level. Clergy staff persons who previously allowed those powerful people to stay on the board while they themselves did the ministry must break two patterns: their own and that of their board.

If lay resistance surfaces during this transition, the reason often is that the "old guard" fear that if they cannot influence who leads the church they will lose control of "their" church.

This diagnosis, which was analyzed in the berry-bucket section of chapter 8, is absolutely right. To grow beyond an attendance of eight-to twelve hundred, a church must have a staff-initiated leadership.

The long process of making this shift, both in attitude and administrative structure, must begin when a church is crossing the four-hundred mark. It must begin to operate in a way that the staff is not driven by a volunteer-controlled board.

Why? At this point the church has become so big that it is no longer practical for part-time workers to manage the church's co-ordination tasks. Too many details arise that cannot wait until the board convenes each month. No matter how efficient the board tries to be, it can regularly bottleneck the staff's efforts to build growth momentum.

Streamlined Church Boards

An increasing number of churches, however, realize that the harvest potential at their doorsteps is enormous. They want to be available to God for whatever doors the Holy Spirit might open. They are willing to be stretched into new roles that will allow for greater growth.

> An increasing number of churches . . . are willing to be stretched into new roles that will allow for future growth.

For such churches, what should be the continuing role of an executive board or governing committee (see Figure 9)?

1. Authorize policy. Policy establishes the basis for standard operating procedures. It helps both pastor and people evaluate whether they are on track in what they are trying to do. It estab-

lishes precedents for operating in a rational and predictable way. It ensures that a church's values are contained in church-planning statements.

Policy, for example, says: Before we purchase this real estate, the following checks will have taken place. Policy may also be general: We will have a written annual plan; we will have a financial audit conducted by an outside accountant; the senior minister, with the appropriate executive staff, will recommend the hiring and firing of all staff, and will inform the board of such actions.

The smaller the church, the more the policy is shaped by the personalities of the people it will affect. The larger the church, the more policy is shaped by the issues involved. For example, the launching of a support-and-recovery ministry might receive impetus in a smaller church from a board member concerned about her wayward son. In the larger church the launching of a new ministry might be guided more by overall plans, objectives, and demographic issues.

Some churches become wrapped up in policy but for the wrong reasons. For example, consider what happens when the pastor or leader is lacking in confrontational skills. I knew of one minister who spent three years guiding his board to rewrite the church constitution, because he could not deal with one difficult elder. You cannot develop effective policy without first having appropriate people skills.

What are the advantages of having a board that authorizes policy? First, it creates a forum for well-placed members to monitor quality-of-ministry issues. They have ears to the ground and can advise the senior leadership on the spiritual health and operational flow of the church.

Second, board members serve as role models. By showing other parishioners what it means to be exemplary lay leaders, they help preserve values that the pastors are building into the church.

Third, this kind of board marks the difference between the senior leadership's thinking out loud and the resulting formalized, approved, officially sanctioned plans. In this way the board's formal role solidifies the planning process.

Finally, the board contributes to a unified vision. If, for example, the senior pastor has difficulty with some aspect of staff manage-

Figure 9

Legitimate Roles and
Goals for Church Boards

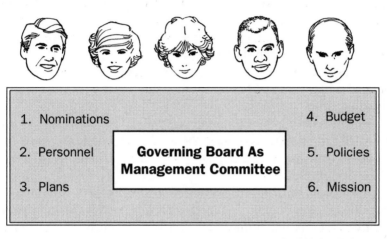

ment, the board can affirm, "We agree with you; take it back and tell the staff to shape it up this way." The staff writes the plan, the board approves it, and the leader guides its formation and approval.

2. Nominate. A board is necessary to designate who does what in the church, especially who sits on key boards and committees. The two groups on the board most critical for steering the direction of the church are typically the nominating committee and the parish-relations committee.

Whenever possible, therefore, the pastor (or a close and loyal friend) should be on these boards. The pastor who seems indifferent to who is part of the nomination process either has no plans to lead the church to size, is incredibly naive, or has a spouse who is well connected politically and in every other sense to the congregation. (This spousal factor cannot be overrated.)

The future tells us that appointment, rather than election, will be the more common way people come to ministry. A church that hands most of its ministry slots to elected positions is on a collision course. Elections too often operate on popularities, not ministry competencies.

3. Select senior staff. When a senior pastor retires, falls, moves, or dies, the board triggers all the mechanisms necessary to secure a replacement. Sometimes the board helps the senior pastor fill other key staff positions. Otherwise, the board should not be very concerned with the hiring and firing of staff. As much as possible, the senior staff will decide staffing issues.

4. Resolve staff conflicts. Church boards spend a lot of time, both in and out of the boardroom, reducing the level of staff infighting.

What causes such widespread staff conflict? Most pastors enter their first multistaff roles with the expectation that they will have no boss. Any attempt to impose "boss-ship" usually results in all kinds of dirty fighting.

In dysfunctional families (which, unfortunately, describes the families of many clergy in North America[1]) even spiritual people behave carnally when they face conflict. To make matters worse, the passive-aggressive personality is probably the character trait most often selected for ministry. The candidate is passive enough for others to think he is controllable or innocuous. But the aggressive side of his character knows how to be angry, deal spitefully, and keep a frustrated or depressive spouse in a state of co-dependency.[2]

If senior pastors do not know when to fire people, and if their staff consistently manifest poor communication skills, the resulting multistaff melee will be a killing ground with a constant undercurrent of conflict. This is where boards have to step in.

5. Implement mission and plans. If a church has a mission statement and direction, boards will want to be part of an active planning process. They prefer that the staff not do it all themselves; they want a sense of ownership. The key is to direct the board's energy and skill into owning and fleshing out the pastor's vision, not wading through the details of implementation.

As deep and wide as the senior pastor's vision is, so goes the organization. If the senior pastor, like Moses, spends time with God on the mountain, the plans that come to the church board will be durable. Mission comes from prayer, from the written Word of God, and from discussion with God's people.

> Mission comes from prayer, from the written Word of God, and from discussion with God's people.

Ultimately, all church mission statements have certain common threads. They contain a vertical dimension such as loving and obeying God. And they emphasize a horizontal dimension: how Christians treat those both inside and outside the church. They answer the question of why God left the church here on earth.

The secret of success is not the wording but the fact that the people of the board have dug the mission statement out of the Bible for themselves, have decided to commit their church to it, and have made it theirs.

6. Approve budgets. Many churches accomplish their planning through a budgeting process. They have not realized that they can create a plan and then match dollars to it. As Lyle Schaller points out, the typical atmosphere in a nongrowing church is a fight over how to split the pie and divide the anticipated spoils. The common scenario is that the board says no to every opportunity that presents itself, and thus the church never has the funds to do the innovative things that are needed.

According to Schaller, the most important shift a board can make is toward an opportunity focus. Lead your board to consider what needs to be done and what God will bless. Then build your budget from that point.[3]

A leader has no power in an organization until he or she can influence a group to say yes. In a church, as in any bureaucracy, virtually no one has the power to say yes. A church board tends to accumulate conservators, thereby gathering in one room the biggest group of potential blockers in the church. What a wonderful opportunity for the pastor to help them turn loose their precious treasure and commit themselves to faith!

Board members often will permit their pastors to take leadership in direct proportion to the pastors' willingness to raise money. And to whatever extent the pastors develop track records for gathering funds, the board will give them freedom to direct the spending of it.

After two to three years of solid financial leadership, the senior pastor can then ask for expenditures without the board becoming uptight. By contrast, when the board has to bail out the pastors' financial decisions, they are very reluctant to grant permission for their leadership to spend more.

This principle holds true in other areas. Do you want to have power to guide your staff? Deal with your own dirty laundry. Handle discipline and conflict within your staff. Show skill in how you dismiss poorly performing staff members, or, more likely, in how you learn to do a better job of supervising them.

What about staff compensation? This issue will probably remain a board decision, but as your church becomes larger, your budget will tend to have a one-line total that reads "salaries," and the breakdown will be created by a personnel committee.[4]

7. Be a safety valve. A board enhances two-way interpretation of program purposes and effects. When people want to complain about how something was handled, the board can say, "No, we talked about that, and here's what we found."

8. Participate in a growth regimen. Laypeople on the main church board will receive special attention from the pastor who promotes their spiritual growth.

Pastors are forever having to ask themselves, "How should I spend my time?" The most strategic answer is to work with leaders, such as your staff and your board. Give them some quality time. They should expect that you will not leave them in the same spiritual condition as when they first came on the board.

How the Management Staff Responds

When the board and committee roles have been clarified, the net result is more executive responsibility for the professional staff. Their role is now to utilize managerial skills for planning, communicating, problem identification, and problem solving. They also must expand their personnel skills in areas of staff selection, assignment, and team building.

What does this look like? First, the senior pastor becomes the primary person who articulates and communicates the vision and accepts responsibility for the oversight of the staff (see Figure 10). This leader paints the picture of the preferred future: what must be done in the long view for effective ministry. He or she solicits the church's commitment to that ideal. This is not done by edict or coercion; rather, vision persuades. The leader creates an enthusiastic and dedicated commitment to a goal, because it is right for the times, right for the organization, and right for the people who are part of the church.

For example, the world's largest church, Yoido Full Gospel Central Church, led by Paul Yonggi Cho in Seoul, Korea, did not develop 55,000 cell-group leaders by accident. They exist, by the grace of God, because Dr. Cho had a vision of what would happen if he would release laypeople to care for one another. He realized that for this to happen he would need to provide them with tools and supervision. So he envisioned one staff member for every fifty cells, and that is exactly what God helped him put in place over time.

Second, the staff members accept roles as being part of a management committee and as overseers of the ministry. They interpret the senior pastor's vision into the how-to's and time frameworks. The staff, then, must be skilled in leadership development, administration, and delegation.

Third, the church board becomes smaller—ideally a single-digit size of one senior pastor plus a handful of administratively gifted laypeople.

Staffing: First Things First

Is there a preferred sequence for adding staff to a growing church? Can certain tools (such as those highlighted in chapter 3, note 10) predict how well a prospective staff member would mesh with the rest of the team?

Yes. Before trying to use those tools, however, the senior pastor must understand a certain role change necessary to be an effective leader of staff: from being a manager to being a leader. What is the

Figure 10

Policy vs. Ministry Hats

© 1992 Carl F. George

difference? Leaders set a direction; managers outline the steps to the destination.

Many of you will have to do both jobs to some extent. But most churches (and businesses) are overmanaged and underled. Pastors are more obsessed with doing things *right* than with doing the right *things.* They give more attention to efficiency than to effectiveness.

A leader gives direction by calling for a vision to come into real-

> Pastors are more obsessed with doing things *right*
> than with doing the right *things*. They give more attention
> to efficiency than to effectiveness.

ity. A manager sees to it that the vision gets accomplished through others. "This is the way to the promised land, and the journey starts right over there," says the leader. Everything else can be done by someone else.

The first step in bringing on new staff is to determine how you will disengage this person in the event the arrangement goes awry. My observation has been that a large-church pastor's first few experiences in hiring lead to a lot of bruising; then he or she copes with the pain by resolving not to hire anyone again.

Instead, pastors learning how to work in a multiple-staff situation need to deal with the root problem, which usually stems from the assignment-and-evaluation process being mucky. If no clear expectations have been set, the level of accountability cannot be focused.

The next step is to select the best candidate. That means taking the time to evaluate at least three nominees. The cost of the interviewing process and of checking multiple references on each person is small compared with the damage, legal and otherwise, that could result if you bring on the wrong person and do not handle the termination swiftly and decently.

Then prepare a description of what you want this next staff member to do. Remember, though, that you will have a harder time getting work out of people than hiring them. While most pastors profit from having clerical or administrative assistance, the tendency is to hire trained, program-staff caliber people and then offer the newcomer no greater opportunity than that of being a sidekick.

Instead, pinpoint the results you want and determine your staff needs accordingly. My recommendation is that you hire leaders to produce new lay leaders. If staff members are not in the business of grooming leaders, then you cannot afford to hire them. A new staff member ought to be able to produce fifty new lay leaders (people who lead others) within a three-year period.

Trends for Today

With this perspective in mind, you are ready to ask what specific roles you want new staff members to fill. The most common pattern today is to start with a senior minister and a part-time secretary. As a church grows, the next position is a minister of education. Soon the secretary works full-time.

By the time a church bumps against an attendance of two hundred, it will have added a part-time minister of youth, a part-time minister of music, and a custodian.

As this common progression continues to a size of three hundred, the youth minister works full-time and an extra part-time secretary has come on board. Interns may become involved at this point. By four hundred the music staff either works full-time or adds part-time assistants, the second secretary works full-time, and the church will add another part-time custodian.

By an attendance of five hundred, a church will have added some specialty associate ministers in various life-stage divisions, such as children, collegians, young adults, or senior adults. As the growth continues, a full-time business manager will be brought on staff.[5]

The ratio, then, breaks down to one pastor for every 100 to 150 people in attendance. The most recent modification in this trend my colleagues and I have observed is that churches tend to bring on more clerical and secretarial staff at an earlier stage. Whereas churches used to hire one secretary for every two program-staff members, the present field wisdom is to employ two secretaries for every one program-staff person.

Is this overall pattern the best way to go? While it contains much wisdom, one flaw cannot be overlooked: It tends to separate the senior minister from the lay-ministry organization of the church. That broken connection is one of the things that accounts for poor performance in many of the churches that I have studied.

In other words, when the senior pastor is not in direct contact with volunteer leaders—the choir directors, Sunday school teachers, head deacons, youth-program people—there tends to be a deficiency of supervision or vision from the senior pastor. Staff, in their middle-man role between senior leadership and lay leaders, tend to insulate the senior pastor's vision rather than translate it.

This dilemma raises a question of delegation: Is vision something that should be left to the staff, or can it effectively be transmitted through the ranks? Increasingly my research shows that organizational hierarchies are being compressed and leaders are finding great benefit from having direct contact with their crew chiefs.[6]

How to Improve Your Delegation Skills

One of the keys to effective leadership is to work from your areas of strength, not weakness. As Peter Drucker, a leading writer in management science, has said, the purpose of organization is to make weakness irrelevant.[7] To maximize what you do best you need to be an effective delegator.

Is the purpose of delegation, then, to get rid of work you do not want to do? Absolutely not. If your primary motive is to develop people, and to develop leaders in particular, then the art of delegation can become a powerful tool in the discipleship process.

To do that you must gain a clear understanding of an important issue: levels of authority. That is, when you decide to delegate something, you need to specify what kind of permission and accountability is expected.

How do you decide what level of delegation is appropriate? Ask yourself. What is the importance of the task you are delegating and to whom are you giving the assignment? The more mature the person, the deeper level you can assign. Also, you might have a highly trusted person but not fully relinquish the responsibility.

How do you determine the layering of authority? The layers posited in literature on management range from three levels to eight.[8] I prefer these six, which move from shallow to deep:

1. Give me a report on the problem, and I'll take action.
2. Study the problem, and make a recommendation.
3. Analyze the situation, propose a course of action that you will take, but wait for my approval.
4. Analyze the situation, describe your proposed plan of action, and follow through unless I say no.
5. Take action, and tell me what you did.
6. Take care of the situation. No need to report back to me.

Our findings are that most leaders and managers know far more about delegating than they act on. Why? As the following self-evaluation moment may well confirm, and the sheepherder-to-rancher theme of this book explains, church leaders have a strong drive to do everything themselves.

Self-Evaluation Moment

How well do you delegate? Take this brief quiz and find out.

Yes No

— — 1. Are you afraid your people will make mistakes?

— — 2. Do you frequently take work home or work late at the office?

— — 3. Does your operation function smoothly when you're absent?

— — 4. Do you spend more time working on details than you do on planning and supervising?

— — 5. Is your follow-up procedure adequate?

— — 6. Do you overrule or reverse decisions made by those on your team?

— — 7. Do you bypass others by making decisions that are part of their jobs?

— — 8. Do you do several things your assistants could, and should, be doing?

— — 9. If you were incapacitated for six months, is there someone who could readily take your place?

— — 10. Will there be a big pile of paper requiring your action when you return from a trip or absence?

To score yourself, add one point for each "yes" answer to numbers 3, 5, and 9, and one point for each "no" answer to numbers 1, 2, 4, 6, 7, 8, and 10. A good score is 8 or above.[9] A score of 5 or below is the normal range for ministers I interview.

The pastor or lay leader who is a rancher understands that some people are empowered by group discussion and chartering, and some people are empowered by a simple "Go for it." Your recognition of the difference between the independent initiative takers and committee-empowered parishioners helps you to make assignments appropriate to the type of persons they are.

Where do you begin? Review your activities of the last week. What percent were ones that only you could do and only you should do?

Next, make a list of all the church responsibilities you have already delegated to other staff members, to clerical assistants, to volunteer workers, and to any others. What additional obligations could you delegate? Which activities are you uncertain about delegating? What activities are you doing that no one, including yourself, should do?

Finally, work through the following self-evaluation moment to pinpoint the delegation-related reasons that prevent you from being a more effective rancher.

Self-Evaluation Moment

What are your greatest obstacles to ranching? Circle the two most important.

1. I don't know how; I was never trained in ranching.

2. I'm fighting a long-standing habit of doing everything myself.

3. My church doesn't expect me to be a rancher or delegator.

4. Frankly, I receive too much ego satisfaction from being needed.

5. I don't ranch, because the job of training laypeople is too hard.

6. I don't ranch, because I feel my laypeople are inadequate.

7. I can't ranch, because my laypeople feel inadequate.

8. I'm unable to find willing workers to whom I can delegate.

9. I'm too insecure to shift from sheepherder to rancher.

10. I don't see ranching as what I'm supposed to do.

What will be your next step in overcoming this barrier?

If you do not delegate effectively, your church's growth will eventually stop. Your fatigue can lead to decisions of such poor quality that you may sabotage yourself. How, then, do you stay rested? Stop doing things that other people could do. Focus your energies on those things that only you can do. Pass the rest of the work to your team. Keep growing in this all-important area.

Self-Evaluation Moment

Each of the following examples could result, if not handled correctly, in an assignment that boomerangs back to the one who delegated it. In each, if you were the pastor, what could you do to make sure the original assignments remained delegated?

1. "We've been having trouble with the heating unit in the family-life center," says one of the trustees to a staff pastor. "I think it needs to be replaced. But before I authorize the expenditure, would you mind having it evaluated?"

2. "I know you don't have time to deal with it now," says the children's director to the minister of education, "but we have a major space-usage conflict between the Sunday school and the Pioneer Girls club. Could you give it some thought and get back to me?"

3. "Pastor," reads a memo from the music director that was left on the pastor's desk during the lunch hour, "please review the enclosed plans for an Easter pageant we'd like to create. I would like to commission the program at our planning committee which meets tonight. Please get back to me before then."

4. "Pastor," says the Sunday school superintendent for the junior-high boys' program, "we keep losing leaders. If we

don't get some help soon, we're going to lose our remaining teachers. I'm out of ideas, so I figured it was your turn now."[10]

Solutions: Set a date with the person to work on the problem together. Decline the request by putting the ball back in the staff person's court. Do not allow staff to give you deadlines without first giving a verbal okay. Clarify lines of responsibility so that each person knows his or her role.

The Challenge Before You

Breaking the 400 barrier may not be for every person or every church. But chances are that many God-gifted people in your church have not yet reached their potential. As a result, a ripened harvest awaits capable leaders who mobilize their laypeople to "go and make disciples of all nations" (Matt. 28:19).

Nothing can substitute for enjoying God for who he is and taking time to smell life's roses. The management insights of this chapter are not intended to suck you into a bottomless vortex of greater activity.

But perhaps God also wants to be a greater part of your ministry and life than he is now. Perhaps God has a greater future for you than you have even begun to imagine. Will you purpose before him to be all that he calls you to become?

For Further Thought

1. How does the development of your church board compare with the pattern described in this chapter? Where are you now? In what ways are you moving or not moving toward the next phase?

2. How distinct and identifiable in your church are the roles of: (1) the chief executive officer and staff, (2) the board, (3) and the ministry leaders? How would your key board members answer that question?

3. If the senior pastor asked you to reshape the function of your church board so that it matched the description found in this chapter, what "hoops" would you need to go through? Which step of the process would be the most sensitive?

4. When your church hired its most recent staff person, by what criteria did you decide on the responsibilities of that person? on the personality strengths needed by that person?

5. What are your strongest skills in delegating? Your greatest areas for improvement? What was the most recent major project you delegated? Did you assign a specific level of authority? What is a recent project that you could have delegated but did not? Why did you not delegate it?

11

How to Break
the 800 Barrier

The greatest challenge facing most North American churches is to break the 200 barrier. The few who breach that attendance level and continue to grow face another critical growth point somewhere between the 600 and 1,200 size.

To cross that hurdle, a church's leaders must continue to hone their ranching abilities. Otherwise problems of ministry will cause too much fatigue and inadequate spans of care will surface. I address both these issues below, because they try to creep in the window of a pastor's office, no matter how large the church becomes.

In general, however, skill sharpening is more the need of leadership trying to move from the 200 barrier to the 800 barrier. A church wanting to increase beyond the 800 barrier must address something greater than proficiency training; it must introduce certain fundamental, significant changes in the church's organizational structure.

One of those changes, the shifting role of the church board, received attention in chapter 10. By the time a church reaches the 800 barrier, the transfer of initiative taking must have left the aegis of the board and been reseated as the domain of the senior staff.

Other necessary changes deal with marketing, facilities usage, and organizational design. This chapter will address each of those issues. First, however, we need to review the ranching idea.

Solve Your Fatigue Problems

What motivates a pastor serving a multistaff church, which ministers to hundreds of people weekly, to come to a seminar entitled "Beyond 800"? Of the more than two thousand ministers who have gone through this conference, which I teach for the Charles E. Fuller Institute of Evangelism and Church Growth, a sizeable number had reached a threshold of pain. They saw themselves on an expressway labeled "Terminal Fatigue" and wanted to know if there is an alternate route to the future.

I trace the roots of their weariness to a stereotype, which at first seems as ludicrous as if we were taking a straw man to task. But most who think through the progression agree that there is more reality in the pattern than they had previously acknowledged.

The story goes like this. In previous generations, the image of a church was one in which the elders (consistory, vestry, deacons, etc.) gathered money in the treasury, went out, and hired a preacher. This employee of theirs delivered the sermon on Sunday and then, during the week, made hospital calls, was available for crises, showed up at the Lions Club to offer a prayer, or otherwise waited for the phone to ring. If there was need for a funeral or wedding, this pastor would be glad to attend to that as well.

The bottom line was that if anything needed to be done for God, the pastor was the hired hand who would do it. If a church did not guard itself, it could become lazy, because its main activity was to give money and vote, while its pastor worked hard and was tired all the time.

Even in churches that learned how to release lay leaders for ministry, the pastors were still expected to do much of the work of the church. Over time, as some churches grew very large, those patterns still remained, even though a lot more volunteers were helping out.

Now, enter the present. In my role as a consultant, I interviewed the staff of a church of 4,500. One of my assignments was to help the church think ahead to the future. So, based on the assumption that the church would continue to grow, I asked what I thought was a logical and predictable question: "What's this church going to look and feel like when it's nine thousand in size?"

The answer was almost a chorus: "Nine thousand?" Everyone's voice carried a tone of disbelief. To underscore their response, one of them confirmed, "That's twice as big as we are now."

After an awkward silence, another staff member finally said, "If twice as big means twice as tired, Lord, let me out now." These people were stressed to the breaking point and could not imagine reaching a greater harvest in their city. They had not yet begun to ranch on a level that allowed them breathing room for managerial and emotional refreshment.

Exceptional Talent and Extra-Mile Dedication

In my observations of large churches, a prime source of ministerial fatigue still traces back to a pastoral staff that operates under the sheepherder model. Whether unwittingly or not, ministers continue to train the parish to expect them to be available in ways that no human can consistently deliver.

As one example, an associate pastor in a church of some 6,000 people bumped into one of the church's long-term members in the hallway on Sunday morning. She confided that she was experiencing the messy breakup of a thirty-year marriage.

After responding with great empathy and concern, the pastor pulled out his appointment book and said, "I want you to know something. As a pastoral counselor on the staff of this church, I am behind you in this tragedy. I am putting your name right here at the very top of my list, and I want you to know that if you need us, we are here."

"Oh," she responded, "that is so comforting. Thank you very much." They prayed together, and she went home.

A few weeks later she had occasion to phone him, but he did not return her call. A couple of days later she left another message, but he still did not call back. After numerous unsuccessful attempts over a couple of weeks, she went to the church building and said to the receptionist, "Is Pastor Such-and-Such in?"

"Yes, but he can't receive any callers."

She nevertheless proceeded down the hall, found his office, walked in, and there was the dear man. On the credenza behind him were thirty-eight pink "While-You-Were-Out" message slips laid out in neat rows.

"Aren't you the same man," she began, "who said to me that because of the great trial I am undergoing and because of your availability to me I would not have to go through this alone? Didn't you put my name in your little black book, and didn't you tell me that you'd return my calls?"

He looked at her and said, "You don't seem to understand. I have thirty-eight calls here. Your call is fifth from the bottom of the pile. I have thirty-three other people I must call before I can get to you. I am working as hard as I know how. I'm putting in twelve-to-fourteen-hour days. I'm covering the territory as quickly as possible, and you'll just have to wait your turn!"

She walked out of his office, shattered and disillusioned. As it turned out, a laywoman in that church filled the need, from helping her deal with malpractice on the part of her attorney, to sitting with her in the courtroom during the long days of the trial, to taking her calls in the middle of the night as she wept her way, hour after hour, through all the adjustments.

Conventional wisdom says that the associate pastor ought to be taken out and flogged. But why? He loves people and genuinely wants to help them; that is why he entered the ministry. He voluntarily puts in overtime, which results in twelve-to-fourteen-hour days, at no extra pay. He was taking very seriously the thirty-eight phone calls that had come his way.

Who was the real victim? Others besides the woman going through the divorce. What about the wife and children of that staff member who, after fourteen hours, came home completely worn out? He was too beat to be a husband or a father. Was not the entire pastoral family a victim as well?

I submit that everyone was a victim, and that no one was the bad guy. I suggest that the villain was not a person but an insane idea that says it is possible for one person to be available to take care of 100, 200, 500, or 800 other people. The casualty was anybody living under that perfectly abominable notion.

What is the implication for a church trying to break the 800 barrier? Even extraordinary talent and extra-mile dedication cannot prevent eventual burnout. The pastor who sets up a sheepherder expectation by repeatedly saying, "Let me be your pastor," will sooner or later be pulled to the point of exhaustion.

A necessary step to break the 800 barrier, the transition point most churches hit between 600 and 1,200, is to continually revise your estimate of what systems are needed to see to it that your people receive the care they need. Remember, your faithfulness or unfaithfulness as a pastor is not measured in terms of fatigue.

The first step toward a solution is to organize your time around delegating duties and training apprentices. Until you become dispensable you cannot become promotable. God cannot hand you a new assignment if it would sink what he has already entrusted to you to oversee.

A second step is to rethink the organizational structure itself. Could improvements be made that would better ensure systemic spans of care?

In the sections that follow, both of these steps will be fleshed out in greater detail.

> Properly managed spans of care are critical
> to a leader's effectiveness.

Establish Reasonable Spans of Care

Properly managed spans of care are critical to a leader's effectiveness. The fundamental message that Jethro gave his son-in-law Moses was the wisdom in breaking an organization into smaller parts so that everyone could have an opportunity to be heard and have his or her questions addressed (see Exod. 18:13–23). A church, therefore, is most effective when it organizes itself around the spans of care that prove to be most manageable.

A lay pastor, under certain conditions, can typically run herd on about twenty names and can keep about ten people coming to a cell group. That assumes (1) the names are not a randomly selected church-provided list but represent an affinity relationship among people already in the group; (2) this layperson has the help of both an apprentice leader and a host who takes care of the meeting location, refreshments, and the like; and (3) this layperson receives coaching, supervision, and encouragement on a regular basis.[1]

If lay ministers try to handle more people than that, they will, in most cases, run out of steam or they will neglect the needs of various members of their group. Once the group size exceeds about thirteen people, it will lose the qualities of intimacy, accountability, pastoral care, hands-on personal prayer, safety in self-disclosure, and surrogate extended-family support that the cell alone can deliver.

Instead, it becomes a class (15 to 25 people) or a congregation (25 to 150 people). General fellowship and a familylike feeling may be present, as well as acquaintance-making opportunities. The leadership will have opportunities to use their own spiritual gifts and train other leaders who are capable of leading additional groups. But neither the class nor the congregation can disciple most people with the quality of care they need.

If a church's goal is to make and multiply disciples of Jesus Christ, then it has two fundamental options: to use the effort and ministry of the professional clergy or to use the lay leadership. If the paid staff are the medium, they will always be weary and short. If an organization of lay volunteers is the medium, the care will be ever expanding and adequate *if* the span of care for each can remain small enough to be effective.

Whom should the leaders in a beyond-800 size church include in their personal spans of care? Other leaders, such as other staff members, the main church board, and those lay volunteers who have taken the responsibility to serve as coaches of lay pastors. By maintaining a leadership development focus within a reasonable span of care, a pastor can both avoid fatigue and continue leading the church to capture new growth opportunities.

Use Niche Marketing to Reach New People

In that regard, imagine that your church begins to experience and sustain a growth rate of ten new people a week. That translates into 400 a year. Five years from now, your cumulative influx will amount to 2,000 new people.

What, on the human level, would be necessary for that to happen? No matter what methodology you use, such as from the list of sixteen methods in chapter 4, you will have to deal with certain stubborn realities to build a bridge between your church and your community.

Here are some general questions to ask as you seek how to unleash your church into your community or regional area:

1. Does your community perceive your church as a source of help? In other words, how does your church position itself in the eyes of the population segment you are targeting?

2. Does your community know who and what your church is? Do you have a clear strategy to interpret your church's program to your most susceptible population segments?

3. Can you scratch that itch? Do you know how to organize the resources of your church in such a way that you can fulfill the expectations of the market segment you are targeting?

4. Do you help people take part? As responding seekers come to church gatherings, what is your pathway for induction? Is there a clear route to membership and/or to greater levels of participation? Does it follow a progression that starts where they are now and that gradually offers them higher challenges and more abundant opportunities for commitment?

5. Do your people experience vital Christianity? How does your church engender spiritual experience and formation? How does each meeting in your church, from the worship service to the senior adult travel club, contribute to this objective? In other words, how do faith, prayer, and other disciplines of the Christian life lead to transformed lives at each meeting these newcomers could be part of?

6. How does your church maintain a quality of community that provides care for all your people? All churches must deal with this issue, especially as they grow larger. How would your church complete the following sentence? "Everyone who wants to receive personal, pastoral-type care may do so through _____." Answers may range from, "We offer one-on-one counseling" to, "We're confident that, with all the programs we offer, you'll stumble upon something that gives you the care you need." I believe that the most workable, long-term solution is an intentional, carefully coached system of lay-led small groups. I introduced this idea in chapter 9 and will expand on it in chapter 12.

One of the privileges of a large church is that it has the talent and resources to market itself to very specific niches of a population. "Bridge events" can target special interests and offer additional entry points to the church. These might include, for example, a seminar offered by a Christian medical doctor on "Seven Keys for Coping with Stress"; a workshop on how to teach English as a second language; a bunch of auto mechanics who get together at a local garage every Friday night, and bring their friends, to do car repairs for widows and others in need; a youth group designed to appeal to the street-wise kids in the housing project down the street from the church building.

You can find several excellent resources that provide numerous insights and principles on marketing;[2] however, one of your goals should be not to advertise your merchandise but to merchandise your advertising. The Sears, Roebuck Company knows that come March, people will want to buy fertilizer for their gardens and spring clothes for their children. So its stores already have the merchandise on display when the need arises. Likewise, a church needs to know its targeted population well enough to have anticipated its felt needs, and be primed, prepared, and programmed to meet those needs in Jesus' name.

Self-Evaluation Moment

1. List twenty-five words or phrases that indicate why someone would want to attend a church.

2. Circle the words or phrases that indicate the felt needs your church is able to meet.

3. Put stars by the words or phrases that would particularly appeal to unchurched or unconverted people.

Divide by Age or Lifestyle

Recognizing the need for increased market targeting, most churches, by about 800, have already begun to re-configure their staffs. In the previous chapter I described how, up to about four hundred people, a church will develop a staff of specialists—a minister of music, of Christian education, or outreach, etc. The larger church typically maintains the concepts of worship, fellowship, and education, but hires staff who will cover all three elements within one age group or life stage.

Each of the staff members, from youth minister to senior-adults minister, receives the same assignment: "See to it that your age group comes to *worship* and has suitable program opportunities for *fellowship* and Christian *education.*" These clergy, if given adequate resources and held accountable, can each carry 150 to 200 people.

They typically sponsor large events, middle-sized gatherings, and small-group meetings. The usual net effect is that each age group or life stage behaves like a little church; it accepts some people and excludes others; it takes good care of some and leaves others in the cold. Typically, more emphasis is placed on the teaching of intellectual concepts and on overall general fraternity than on the creation of intentional community.

A church such as this centers on the necessity of the congregation-sized structure, and it offers cells and classes as "nice to have" but not as necessities. Likewise, the celebration is a festival or convention of congregations, not a gathering of cells. The age- and life-stage targeting is healthy; the questionable notions are whether the congregation-sized group can be a primary-care structure or whether the congregation-sized group can be a significant entry port to the growth of the celebration.

The clergy of a congregation-centered church, though all quite busy, usually lack a purposeful plan for developing their lay leaders. The organizational chart for their church usually offers limited insight into who supervises whom, because it lists only the paid staff and identifies their relationship to the senior pastor or church board. As a result, a volunteer or part-time director of preschool ministry may oversee a staff that handles five hundred people, while the main responsibility of an ordained minister of singles may be one thirty-five person class.

My point is not to demean someone whose ministry is smaller than another's (or to be anticlerical). Rather, I am highlighting the inefficiency that is frequently a part of this commonly accepted paradigm.

Another problem this type of church faces is that of structural fatigue. As a church continues to grow and begins to minister to thousands of people weekly, it will usually implement a matrix formula in which specialists support the generalists. For example, a minister of evangelism (specialist) will be brought on board who is assigned to support all the ministers of age level (generalists) in developing outreach training and programming for their particular church-within-the-church.

In charting this progression (which I do in greater detail in my book *Prepare Your Church for the Future*[3]), and then researching it in hundreds of actual churches through my work with the Charles E. Fuller Institute of Evangelism and Church Growth, I have discovered that somewhere around 6,000 people, and perhaps as high as 12,000, the pastors fatigue out and the church stops growing. In other words, the popularly used organizational formulas lead to most churches stalling somewhere between 6,000 and 12,000 as if they were a species of shrub that had reached its maximum height (see Figure 11).

Understand the Limits of Superchurches and Megachurches

As a result of faith, guts, and a feeder-receptor system (which will receive further comment in chapter 12), North American soil now boasts more than a thousand churches known as superchurches[4] that have attendances between 1,000 and 3,000, and about 150 churches even larger known as megachurches.[5] Only a handful have consistently broken the 10,000 mark, and no one has sustained growth beyond 20,000.

Indeed, an increasing percentage of North American churches are becoming four-digit entities. According to Lyle Schaller, between 1950 and 1990, the number of Protestant churches averaging 800 or more at worship has at least tripled and perhaps quintupled.[6] Such breakthroughs are reshaping the ecclesiastical landscape. Approximately one-fifth of churches on this continent account for one-half of all Protestant churchgoers.[7]

Enough evidence is on hand to guide any church of 1,000 along this same path. How can you do it according to the currently used pattern highlighted in the previous chapter? (1) Rationalize your marketing by positioning your church as a source of help to a sus-

Figure 11

Ceilings and Choice Points

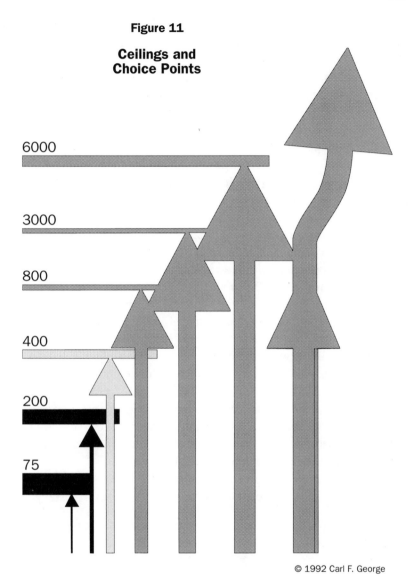

© 1992 Carl F. George

ceptible target population. (2) Manage your programming through giving age and life-stage assignments to your staff, and get the staff—rather than the board—to accept responsibility for planning and budgeting. (3) Shift your focus from that of a sheepherder to that of rancher. I have discussed this latter idea in virtually every chapter of the book, with this very specific recommendation: Put the primary-care pastoral ministry of the church into the hands of lay sheepherders who lead small groups.

These steps, prayerfully applied and directed by the Holy Spirit, can carry you beyond 1,000, but not without an eventual slowdown.

Could there be, however, an alternate path to the future that does not have the same theoretical size limits built in? What if, for example, each age-group or life-stage pastor were commissioned to focus his or her energies on developing a handful of lay leaders who would, in turn, coach a handful of lay leaders who would, in turn, care for the pastoral needs of that particular age group?

Likewise, in the arena of corporate worship, what if a minister of celebrative arts were given the responsibility to produce lay ministry teams who would, in turn, lead the worship?

In other words, each of these pastors will be hired as a producer of other ministers rather than as a performer or primary care giver (other than to a handful of lay leaders). As but one application: Instead of having a minister of evangelism, now every staff member will be responsible for evangelism in every cell, because every cell is responsible for the evangelism of the people it assimilates.

The real church, then, is the cell. Even the worship service is cell driven in that it is a convention of cells. In this kind of church, a small group is not an add-on, like a new corner in a department store, to complement the youth department and the women's ministries department. Rather, the cell is the center of activity, and everything else is rationalized around it.

This modification of structure, I believe, unlocks the terminal fatigue syndrome and uncaps the lid on maximum church size.

> The real church, then, is the cell . . .
> and everything else is rationalized around it.

Offer Multiple Worship Services

The simple question, Should we go to a second (or third, or fourth) worship service? frequently opens the door to a host of related questions: What is the ideal size for our church? Do we want to expand our present ministries, extend ourselves through daughter churches, or both? Would our ministers and choir have the stamina for another service, or would other personnel be needed to fill the leadership spots? What long-cherished traditions and worship styles will be interfered with by an additional service?

Why go the multiple-worship-service route? Consider the following benefits:

1. You will allow the Holy Spirit, more than the city fathers, to determine how great a harvest your church can reach. Not only will you overcome the vision limiter of "a full building means the harvest is complete for this year" (see chapter 2), but you will also circumvent the "no more growth" edicts of your zoning board when you try to enlarge your physical plant.

2. You will position yourself for growth, especially if the additional service "off loads" the better attended 10:30 or 11:00 service. Lyle Schaller calls the multiple-service approach "the most effective means for increasing worship attendance."[8] John Vaughan says that 85 percent of growing churches are in what can be called a multiservice model.[9]

3. You will exercise optimal stewardship of the tens of thousands and even millions of dollars currently invested in your present facilities. Most church facilities are used, at best, at 20 percent of capacity. Josh Hunt, a staff pastor at Calvary Baptist Church, a Southern Baptist church in Las Cruces, New Mexico, calculated, based on 1988 property value figures, that his denomination spent $12,058 for each new member added in the average church. John Vaughan says: "My annual research of the 500 fastest-growing churches in the U.S. indicates that the wiser decision is to use the same space for a second, and then begin a third hour, if at all possible, before completing additional new buildings.[10]

4. You will give additional laypeople a forum for ministry. Many times new talent cannot emerge, because someone is already sitting in a given slot.

Instead of asking the same ushers to do double duty, why not discover how many new people would step forward to usher? Instead of recycling the chancel choir and regular instrumentalists, cultivate a handbell choir, a youth choir, a single-adults a cappella group, a children's glee club. Give them nonprime-time exposure, and then when you feel both they and the congregation are ready, utilize them in your additional services. Lyle Schaller confirms that for every 150 people in attendance, you have enough talent to develop an additional choir.[11]

Does the physical plant of your church stand idle on Thursday night, Friday night, Saturday night, or Sunday afternoon? If a spiritual awakening came over all the unchurched people within a fifteen-minute drive of your church building, and they came to your church for help, you would need all kinds of alternate-hour services.

I propose that the missing ingredient in developing multiple worship services is not the lack of new people but the lack of compelling drive to reach an enlarged harvest, the lack of vision in how to raise enough lay talent to staff the additional services, and the lack of effective leadership that can do the political maneuvering necessary to rally the church in support of such new outreach.

Jack Hyles led First Baptist Church, Hammond, Indiana, to be the nation's largest church; it has held up to six rounds of Sunday school each Sunday. Willow Creek Community Church, South Barrington, Illinois, offers weekend services designed for the seeker at the pace of two on Saturday night and two on Sunday morning, and then weeknight services designed for the believer on both Wednesday night and Thursday night. St. Stephen's Episcopal Church, Sewickley, Pennsylvania, accommodates its weekly attendance of 1,300 by providing five Sunday morning services at seventy-minute intervals beginning at 7:45 A.M. Other churches hold several morning services and then host a Vietnamese, Korean, or Hispanic afternoon service.

The path to the future is already within your grasp, including your present financial resources. Who will step forward and grasp these wonderful opportunities?

Are You Closer to the Future?

Leadership development is the core perspective for the ongoing health and growth of the larger church (see Figure 12). Disciples,

> Leadership development is the core perspective
> for the ongoing health and growth of the large church.

not customers, are made a dozen or less at a time. Jesus' scenario was to pick twelve, fail one, and graduate eleven.

When you analyze the needs of your church or when you plan for the future, do you think primarily of individuals working alone or of an organizational grid that connects individuals through affinity-based groups? Do you see your church as a cluster of influence centers, each of whose particular ministry is shaped, guided, and directed by a specific leader?

The cell system in most churches is like the bin in my refrigerator the week seedless grapes go on sale, and my children have raided the kitchen ahead of me. All I can find are some loose grapes rolling around.

The cell system that takes a church beyond 800 is what the vegetable bin looked like before my children arrived. It was overflowing with grapes and "structured" in such a way that when one of my kids grabbed an appropriate stem in the right place, virtually everything came with it.

Once you understand how all the "grapes" (representing affinity-based groups) plug in to one another at your church—how lay coaches hold each cluster together and how the staff are the stems that connect the clusters one to another—then you have a system to which you can provide effective guidance. Otherwise you are stuck dealing with loose grapes one at a time.

If God is calling your church to be several times larger than you have previously imagined it could be, then you will plateau or stumble if you have to deal with one "grape" at a time. You need to find the stem on which a new social architecture can be constructed. You need a new set of tools to cope with the larger set of realities that you will soon experience.

The good news is that this tool set exists, it is as timeless as the principles of Scripture, and it is being modeled by a number of very exciting churches. The next chapter of this book both describes and names that "new" paradigm.

Figure 12

Developing Leaders

Your name and position

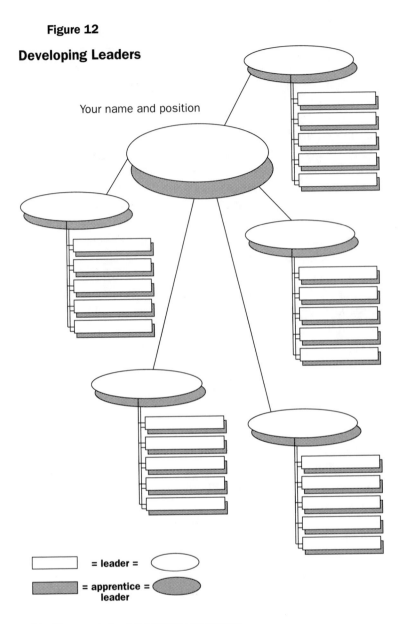

☐ = leader = ⬭

▓ = apprentice = ⬬
leader

Identify your role in all the groups you oversee.
Where are the leadership gaps?
Which positions are highest priority for apprenticeship training?

Leadership development is the core perspective for the ongoing
health and growth of the larger church.

© 1992 Carl F. George

For Further Thought

1. What are the evidences of ministry fatigue in your church? If God grants you an enlarged harvest, what needs to happen to prevent staff and key lay leaders from totally burning out?

2. How do you feel about the concept of "marketing" a church? In what ways could the publicity now generated by your church (brochures, radio broadcasts, Yellow Pages advertisements, streetside signs to promote vacation Bible school) be interpreted as marketing? What is the next step your church needs to take in its overall strategy to build bridges with the unchurched and unconverted?

3. Think of a beyond-800 size church with which you are fairly well acquainted. Is it closer to being an undifferentiated mass unified around the charisma of the main pastor, or an age-based or lifestyle-based set of churches within the big church? Why?

4. If your church has considered or implemented a multiple-worship-service format, what were the biggest snags in launching it? What is the greatest perceived benefit? What would need to happen for your church to launch and fill one more worship service than it is conducting now?

12

How to Break the Care Barrier

What is the next stage for the growing North American church? Some churches plant daughter churches, spin off satellite groups, or add multiple campuses, and yet they continue to maintain their numerical momentum. Some churches experience a change in pastors, or they incorporate a preaching-team approach to ministry, and they still keep increasing in scope.

Is it possible that these churches will break all North American records to date and create a new class that ranges in size from 30,000 to 300,000? If such churches did exist in the Western world, what would be their appeal?

Here is what Christian trend spotters observe as they paint a picture of the future.

Today's North American superchurches and megachurches will be dwarfed by Meta-Churches that support "100,000 to 300,000 members" through an "incredibly personal . . . connectedness at the small-group level" (Russell Chandler, a former pastor who spent seventeen years as an award-winning religion writer at the *Los Angeles Times,* in his book *Racing Toward 2001*).[1]

Just over half of America's adults will *not* attend a church worship service this week.[2] Yet one in four unchurched people (those who do not attend at all in a typical month) would be in church this weekend if a friend were to invite them.[3] (George Barna, President, Barna Research Group, author of *The Frog in the Kettle, What Americans Believe,* and other paradigm-diagnosing resources).

Fifty-eight percent of unchurched adults in the United States (those who neither belong to a church nor visited one in the last six months, except for holidays, weddings, or funerals) said they are open to joining a church if they find the right one (George Gallup, perhaps America's premier pollster, in "The Unchurched American").[4]

More than one analyst has asked, "If the fields are so ripe, what's gone wrong with the harvest?" Why are 80 percent or more of United States and Canadian churches plateaued or declining?[5] Why does the average local church "face a tenuous future"[6] in an increasingly pluralistic and secular environment?

The Holy Spirit Is Being Underutilized

Our lack of greater impact stems, in part, from a widespread mistaken notion that I have tried to challenge in chapter after chapter of this book: that Western Christianity, from long-term church member to lifetime denominational executive, assumes that one person, because of an educational degree or an ordination certificate, is therefore rendered capable of meeting the spiritual and emotional needs of one hundred or more people. This sheepherder or congregation-sized paradigm is a primary mechanism by which the Western church prevents itself from being a fully effective agent of God's redemption for our time.

Even Jesus acknowledged that a better system is needed. He told his disciples, "It is for your good that I am going away. Unless I go away, the Counselor will not come to you" (John 16:7). Jesus shifted his own ministry from that of person-to-person to a ministry of God-in-all-through-the-Holy-Spirit. On another occasion he promised, "Where two or three come together in my name, there am I with them" (Matt. 18:20).

The gift of the Holy Spirit makes it possible for a pastor to have confidence that the love, nurture, encouragement, and care God wishes for people to receive is available each time the Christian community comes together, whether that meeting is convened by ordained clergy or lay shepherds.

When you consider further the idea that each Christian is specially gifted by the Holy Spirit for the one-another ministry that builds up and matures the church (1 Cor. 12:1–12; 14:12, 26), then a new paradigm can be born. I propose that the church of the future—the church that wants to break the care barrier—will have this conviction at its heart: Wherever Christians cluster together, the presence of Christ is there, and adequate grace will be manifest to meet the needs of everyone present. In short, care for unlimited numbers of people is possible, because Jesus designed a better plan.

Many North American churches have acknowledged the importance of small-group, need-meeting intimacy and accountability, from John Wesley's class meetings, to the nineteenth-twentieth-century Sunday school movement, to the cell-church and small-group groundswell[7] evident today. But only the leaders of the pack—the world's largest churches (some twenty churches of over 30,000)[8] and many of North America's largest and fastest growing churches[9]—have applied this perspective to their overall organizational structures.

Badge of Discipleship: One-Another Love

How does a church prepare for an expanded availability of quality care? What structures best help a church flesh out Jesus' teaching that "by this all men will know that you are my disciples, if you love one another" (John 13:35)?

One option is to hire more staff and clergy. Predictably, most churches run out of money long before they run out of needs. In fact, churches below one hundred in attendance will mostly wind up, over the next decade, being led by self-supporting, bivocational clergy. Economics will force it.

On top of that, the ratio of ministers to the total United States population is 1 to 714,[10] hardly a feasible span of care, even if we could double or triple the current number of ordained ministers.

How about training laypeople to serve as paraclergy on a volunteer basis, akin to the Stephen Series of one-to-one caregiving created by Kenneth Haugk?[11] While this wonderful pastoral care concept extends the professional ministry by patching holes in the system, it serves more as a crisis measure than as a long-term answer.

> Care for unlimited numbers of people is possible,
> because Jesus designed a better plan.

The best solution, which enables the largest number of people to receive personal, quality attention, occurs when a church systematizes care by building it into the ongoing life of the entire fellowship. For this to happen, self-help caring must be developed as a mutual resource through a churchwide system of lay-led small groups. This idea echoes the solution to the "disaster area" analogy introduced at the beginning of chapter 1.

In short, the more caring cells your church has, the more people you can sustain and the more crises you can handle without loss of quality. That means more people who will be able, in the name of Jesus Christ, to love a lost world and bring it to the Savior.

Adequate caring lies at the foundation of all sound church growth.

> Adequate caring lies at the foundation
> of all sound church growth.

Why Be Part of a Big Church?

The only reason a church can grow to a five- or six-digit size is that its people receive better care than they would in a smaller church. Its clergy have long ago abandoned the idea that they are the only, or even the best, primary care givers. Such churches are, instead, organized around lay pastoral skills.

As a result, a second raison d'être is born: If someone has hopes of being a lay minister, this kind of church will not only allow him or her to do so, but it will encourage and challenge lay pastoring. The professional clergy will make it clear that the true heroes are lay people, recruited and trained from within the church, who take responsibility for flocks of about ten. These lay pastors will ensure the spiritual nurture of the people in their cells in four ways: (1) They convene the group at least twice a month; (2) they set a tone in the group that conveys an openness to newcomers; (3) they, with the help from an apprentice leader, make sure their people receive care from one another outside the meetings; and (4) they meet regularly with someone who coaches them on their various leadership questions or difficulties.

By contrast, the current North American phenomenon of the superchurch (1,000 to 3,000) and megachurch (3,000 to 20,000) can be traced in most cases to a feeder-receptor pattern of transfer growth from smaller churches.[12] Some 80 percent of all growth taking place in superchurches and megachurches comes through transfer, not conversion.[13]

> Some 80 percent of all the growth taking place
> in superchurches and megachurches
> comes through transfer, not conversion.

I predict that the cell-driven church will have just the opposite experience. People who desire anonymity will be fed into smaller-sized churches that emphasize, instead of cells, one or more congregation-size groups, such as a large adult Bible fellowship or a 150-person singles group.

As Paul Yonggi Cho, pastor of the world's largest church (625,000), which traces its growth to the work of the Holy Spirit through some 55,000 trained lay pastors, explains:

> The large church, through use of small groups, has proven to be uniquely able to be used by the Holy Spirit in our times. People in the small groups minister to each other in ways that they would ordinarily not. . . . And knowing they are all a part of the larger church gives each person a feeling of being a part of an ongoing work of God.[14]

> I firmly believe that when any church adopts this system of home cell groups, it is going to grow.[15]

Prepare Your Church for the Future

Is there a name for a church organized around lay pastoral skills? This concept, which according to *Christianity Today* is "the most prominent on the contemporary church growth scene,"[16] is gaining widespread recognition as the Meta-Church.

What does the term *Meta-Church* signify? One of the people who critiqued *Prepare Your Church for the Future,* the book I wrote to explain the Meta-Church paradigm, said, "You're trying to describe what's coming next."

Exactly. Just as *meta*morphosis is the change of the caterpillar to butterfly, so *Meta-Church* emphasizes the changing character of the church and the new things that God is bringing to pass.

The term was coined to alert leaders to the radical differences in how ministry must be configured to deal with significant changes occurring in societies worldwide. The most fundamental of those alterations is the biological family that is not functioning well, where people are increasingly unable to find support, acceptance, belonging, positive role modeling, and a sense of normalcy.

The prefix *meta*, meaning "change," emphasizes a change in order or pattern in how the members of the family of God relate to one another. It also represents a significant shift in how ministry is perceived: that the clergy's critical task is leadership formation (developing sheepherders and other ranchers) rather than doing hands-on, primary-care ministry (being a sheepherder). Finally, the term *Meta-Church* also represents an accompanying change in organizational priorities and structures.

What does a Meta-Church look like? It is a growing, usually multistaff, local church committed to a joyous corporate worship of God (celebration), to formation of nurture groups and ministry teams (cells) led by lay pastors, and to an organization of professionals and volunteers that focuses on development of leadership for ministry.

Is it any particular size? The Meta-Church concept represents a comprehensive approach to social architecture. It can begin at any attendance level.

How does it grow? In a Meta-Church, evangelism and discipleship become increasingly "cell driven" as believers use gifts of the

Holy Spirit for one-another ministry through affinity-based, self-reproducing small groups. The Meta-Church paradigm allows unlimited numerical expansion without sacrificing quality; it is large enough to celebrate and small enough to care.

Why should a Meta-Church exist? Is the objective to break the 20,000 barrier or to conform to some new, Third World definition of a successful church?

Meta-Churches are *not* motivated by size but to minister to hurting people (see Figure 13). Christians must not be satisfied as long as there is anybody who goes to bed at night crying himself or herself to sleep because of not knowing God's love. If we have to create larger churches, and even fill the landscape with 20,000-size churches for everyone to have an opportunity to be cared for, then that's one of the consequences of living as part of a world population of 5.3 billion people today, 6.3 billion by the year 2000, and 10 billion by the year 2050.[17]

As long as there is one person outside the fold, we cannot rest easy.

> As long as there is one person outside the fold,
> we cannot rest easy.

How Programmatic Thinking Skews Our Focus

Most people, including myself, would agree that the teaching in both mainline and evangelical churches in North America today is, taken as a whole, probably the finest quality of any time in history. We are blessed with more tools, skills, and resources, and a higher level in clergy education than in any previous era.

Rarely does a church exhibit a deficiency in teaching ability. Sometimes we find an inadequacy in teaching priority but not in aptitude.

Learning, however, is a different matter. North American pastors, lay leaders, and congregants believe many things to be true, which, when examined closely, cannot be supported. This misinformation

Figure 13

**A "New" Approach
to Social Architecture**

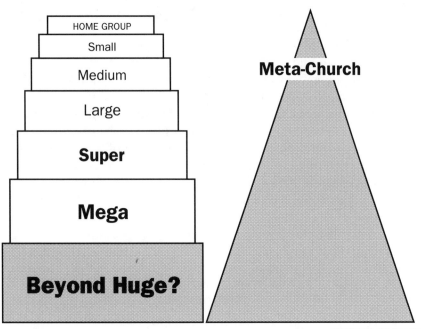

© 1992 Carl F. George

has little to do with the content of the Bible, the person of Jesus Christ, or other foundations to our grounding in God and in faith. Rather, our methodological truths sometimes undermine the passion and doctrine that motivate them.

In short, I believe that the educational process of today's church is far more shaped by American philosophies and methods of traditional public education than by the principles of Holy Writ. As such, a new paradigm, such as what Meta-Church thinking represents, cannot take root until people unlearn some of the programmed, curriculum-based assumptions at the core of North American ecclesiology.

I propose that the chief quality of an effective small-group leader, and, in fact, the heartbeat of that cell ministry, is not the programmed organization or curriculum but a highly relational organism that stems from a person-to-person kind of ministry.

> The chief quality of an effective small-group leader. . . is not the programmed organization or curriculum.

For example, at Eastside Foursquare Church, a Seattle-area fellowship widely respected for its excellent corporate worship services and its felt-needs approach to the baby-boomer generation, Pastor Doug Murren and his staff became aware of the need to establish a network of surrogate extended families among their constituency. So they put out a call asking who would like to be referred to a cell ministry.

Of the then 4,300 regular worship attenders, 1,300 said yes. This response put the church staff into a mild panic as they began to ferret out the possible new lay leadership and extend the present lay leadership to cover these 1,300 searching people. They needed 130 groups of 10, convened in such a way that people could ask questions that left them vulnerable and reveal their inner pain with a depth unachievable in an impersonal large-group setting.

How did the leadership at Eastside handle the situation? Had they followed the normal programmed thinking to which most North Americans are accustomed they would have decided that teachers have very little to do with enrollment, except to record the names and numbers of pupils who come to preassigned classrooms. They would have said, "We'll ask our computer, based on zip-code groupings, to allocate ten people to this teacher and ten people to that teacher."

Though perhaps unintentionally, they would have disrespected who their people were. If someone had consequently dropped out or declined to participate, the church would have sent out an ecclesiastical truant officer rather than ask why its system failed. Such thinking, although amazingly widespread, can treat human beings like pieces of furniture that can be assigned to a place. It can terribly depersonalize people, in my opinion.

Instead, what Eastside Foursquare did was to introduce the Meta-Church paradigm, which is based not on *organization* thinking but on *organism* thinking. In their deployment of leaders, they respected affinity and personal chemistry. Rather than start with a curriculum to be taught or a particular room in their building to be filled and hope that the bonding would be right so that true kinship would emerge, they pursued a far different course. They understood that effective leadership gathers the people and sees to it that they receive care. So they released the leaders to contact and recruit the people.

In short, the core issue in meeting these 1,300 people's needs was whether affinity-based, person-to-person relationships were foundational or incidental. Is a cell group a living organism in which human beings are nurtured and character developed, or is it an organization that can be run whether or not interpersonal relationships are present? The significance of this difference cannot be overestimated.

Why Not Merely "Append" Small Groups to the Present Structure?

Some churches offer small groups as one more option in a supermarket of choices, much as a grocery store creates an extra aisle to feature the latest fads in appetizers or gourmet desserts. In many cases, the cell ministry quickly fizzles or is replaced by the next program in vogue within the denomination or at the nation's high-visibility churches.

The notion of lay-led cell groups is neither new nor unusual. However, they are not a program but a seminal component of a church's vitality and health. The reorientation of a pastor's priorities is not a cosmetic change to updating the marquee in front of the church building or reprinting the church bulletin with a new sermon title.

The shift from programmatic to relational, from a one-size-fits-all to a diagnostic emphasis, can be compared to a total rewiring of the electrical circuits in a church building. Only by a major shift in paradigm will churches begin to send messages to places they have not previously gone or reward values and behavior they have not previously championed.

The journey to the church of the future that is longest, hardest, and yet most important begins in the pastor's mind. Learning to visualize how a church looks from the bottom up requires a dramatic shift in thinking. But the more specific the mental picture, the more able the pastor will be to empower the system to empower the people to be tools in the hand of God (see Figure 14).

> The journey to the church of the future that is the longest, hardest, and yet most important begins in the pastor's mind.

Whatever the pastor's vision is, people will catch it. A fuzzy concept translates into a foggy game plan. A clear, driving passion will be figured out by the key people of a church, even if the pastor does not articulate it.

The Critical Event at Your Church

What is the locus of ministry in your church? The Western church seems infatuated with the altar, the pulpit, and the chairs surrounding the ordained minister as the epitome of "real" ministry. The Meta-Church suggests that the great harvest to which Christians are called requires a new location for the "critical event" in the life of a church.

Take the McDonald's hamburger chain as an illustration. To organize a successful McDonald's restaurant, two important steps must take place. First, a would-be franchiser has to be shown that it makes sense to invest in McDonald's. Otherwise this financier will not put up the capital necessary to erect the building. Second, the franchiser must be trained to make the counter person a hero in the system.

The general public has no contact with the franchiser. In fact, they have no interest in the name or personality of anyone in management. The person who makes a difference to their world is the someone who stands behind the counter and says, "How may I help you?"

Figure 14
Are You "Creaming" Your Leadership—
Or Developing It?

	Typical *"Creaming"* Paradigm	Meta-Church *Development* Paradigm
How New and Expanding Ministry Needs Are Filled	1. Persuade over-burdened saints to wear more "hats" (unless they burn out first). 2. Attract preprocessed Christians from other churches. 3. Create alliances/deals between various age-group leaders (such as between youth director and middle-adult director).	1. Create a leadership development apparatus for each group within the church. Target new believers and relatively inactive "warehoused" Christians.
Resultant Size of Church Volunteer Pool	Fixed—Limited to number of already-trained Christians in your community (your church plus all other area churches).	Ever Expanding—Limited only by the size of the church's "harvest" vision.
Typical Profile of Primary Volunteer Pool	Nesting-stage parents, especially those with children ages 3-15.	Nesting-stage parents, especially those with children ages 3-15.

How Staff Hiring Sequence Impacts This Primary Volunteer Pool	Departmentalizing Pattern:
	1. Youth
	2. Children
	3. Sr. adults (if an older church)
	4. Single adults
	5. THEN: Single parents
	   Young parents
	   Middle parents
	   Empty-nest parents
		Districting Pattern:
		1. Whichever age group has **most** cell-group participants (Typically it's the nesting-stage parents).
		2. Whichever age-group has the **second-most** cell-group participants, etc.
		3. Whatever responsive segments are present in the service area.

Net Results	1. Primary volunteer pool gets overlooked. 2. Small "zero sum" pool of volunteer candidates (i.e., the number of those who attend your church).	1. Primary volunteer pool receives most attention 2. Huge "zero sum" pool of volunteer candidates (i.e., the population of the service area compared to the number of group leaders your church has developed).

Thus the one role in the whole McDonald's system that most determines whether or not you will return is that of the counter person.

The critical event in the entire McDonald's chain, as far as the customers are concerned, is the five-minute wait from the time they hit the door until they walk away with their steaming hot cheeseburgers or fries. (I assume a constant in the quality of the food.)

In other words, if you stand at that stainless steel counter, receive what you asked for, and then leave with your need met within your monetary budget and time limit, you will come back again. Likewise will millions of other people who experience the same favorable results. As far as you are concerned, you do not care what happens in the boardroom or at the franchiser fair. The entire McDonald's system is engineered to see to it that the counter person can deliver what you expect.

I believe churches could create a similar locus of ministry, which could impact the North American consumer in a similarly positive and appealing manner. What if your church's goal were that every person within the influence of your community had the opportunity to be in touch with about ten other people, both in one-on-one experiences and in the context of a small, loving, caring group? That encounter would open the door to a natural progression. When people are able to develop trust and feel well treated, they conclude, "If this group of people is able to love me as unloving as I am, then the God who sent them must be a loving, personal God, too."

The Meta-Church takes the most plentiful talent we have—one person in ten—and asks that individual, by the aid of the Holy Spirit in mutual ministry of the saints, to provide a safe place for people to come to Christ, to ask their questions, to grow, to confess their sins, to find absolution, and to find encouragement. That is the critical event. Everything else in the system had better contribute to it.

The critical event in a Meta-Church, then, revolves around the intimacy of the family unit or spiritual-kinship unit facilitated by a lay minister who has a limited span of care (about ten people) and who has access to training in the social and leadership skills necessary to pull this off and to replicate himself or herself through an apprentice.

That means the baker, the truck driver, the salad maker, the franchiser, the shift leader, and the personnel at McDonald's corporate headquarters must not lose sight of the fact that the critical event must be supported.

Am I suggesting that the pulpit event is no longer necessary? No. A message, even a scholarly one, can be very helpful in identifying and understanding the truths of Scripture.

While the role of the sermon is significant, it stands in the same relationship to the critical task of caring as a franchiser stands in relation to the McDonald's counter person. It is a necessary step, but not the only one. Preaching, therefore, is not the end of your responsibility and thus cannot be considered the only critical event in the life of a church.

The fruit of a Meta-Church pastor is not the shepherd's role of helping another Christian, but the rancher's role of forming another Christian into a leader who, in turn, is capable of training another leader. This is precisely the concept that Paul teaches his apprentice in 2 Timothy 2:2.

In other words, a Meta-Church pastor will shepherd other shepherds: the staff and volunteer leaders who can, in reciprocal fashion, reproduce themselves in others. Through the process dozens, hundreds, and even thousands of others receive pastoral care. That is what ranching is all about.

Enter the Future Now

In the first four printings of my book *Prepare Your Church for the Future,*[18] I perpetuated the popular notion that more people are alive today than have lived in the entire combined history of humanity. Careful population scientists point out that, although no one can be certain, this statistic is not consistent with the best mathematical demography and other available research tools.[19]

Even so, we can be confident that the number of people who do *not* claim to be Christians is numerically greater today than at any other period of recorded history.[20] Translation? The harvest fields are just outside our door as never before.

The next person or ten people, or one hundred, or one thousand who come to Christ in the context of your church could be the finest and most leadership-skilled saints you will ever have the privilege of training. Much will depend on whether you decide to ranch them or to shepherd them.

Consider this as your prayer and resolution: "Dear God, which people in my community would you be pleased to draw to yourself through the enfolding arms of our church? I will, by your grace, see to it that every person who comes our way has the opportunity to be well cared for in a group of no larger than ten. I will pay the price to train and multiply the number of cell-group leaders necessary so that these newcomers can be personally encouraged and matured in their walk with you."

If that prayer reflects the intention of your heart, I predict you will see a transformation in your ministry and in the lives of your people that exceeds any dream you have been able to put together to this point.

The reason? You no longer attempt on the basis of your availability, to be a superpastor, superstaff member, or super lay leader. Instead, your vision is that of tapping into the gift of the Holy Spirit, who indwells every believer in your church. You will confidently seek out and train those people who have been given by God the leadership ability to nurture the spiritual lives of newcomers. And you will work with them to develop the apprentices necessary for the next generation of leadership.

If church leaders can firmly grasp this idea, they can evangelize our cities to the very margins. The follow-up gaps will disappear. The alienation and despair that people now feel will be transformed into hope and confident lives of faith. And broken and wounded families will be rebuilt as people are reparented in the context of spiritual kinship groups.

The net result is that you will experience a blessing from God that exceeds anything you have ever hoped for, imagined, or dared to pray for.

Are you asking God to break the growth barriers in your church? Do you have the capacity to believe that you are capable of leading growth in your church? As soon as you get the answers to those questions straight, your church will grow.

It is as simple—and as hard—as that.

For Further Thought

1. What concept in this chapter registers most deeply with your spirit? Which do you find to be most troublesome?

2. Is the Holy Spirit being underutilized in your church? Why or why not?

3. Have you read about, visited, or known of a Meta-Church? What ministries are you aware of in your community that are in the early stages of changing over to this paradigm?

4. What is the situation in your church at present as to whether preaching is the critical event or lay pastoring is the critical event? How would the McDonald's illustration apply to the structures of your church?

5. As a result of reading and praying through this book, what is God calling you to do and to be? Why? What is the next step for you to take?

Resources

We are committed to helping increase the size and number of Christ-
ian churches—especially through conversion growth. This requires
that we promote the most effective practices of leadership develop-
ment for church growth and evangelism. Therefore, we continually
seek to discover, evaluate, and disseminate knowledge of the most
effective practices and to facilitate their adoption.

That statement describes the mission of the Charles E. Fuller Institute of Evangelism and Church Growth, one of North America's largest in-service trainers of pastors and lay leaders.

It is evident to us at the Institute that a new era in the history of the Church is emerging, and we are exploring every new vista that the Holy Spirit seems to be opening. We will continue to supply quality leadership development material, through books (our hundreds of titles include such current topics as "Recovery Ministries" and such hard-to-find topics as "Large Church"), monthly cassette clubs (*Meta*Facts©, *Shared Ministry* and *The Pastor's Update),* and seminars (we sponsor fifty-plus events, including "How to Break the 200 Barrier," "Beyond 400," "Beyond 800," and "Training Lay Leaders of Home Cell Groups").

At the same time, we are breaking new ground by helping growth-minded churches mentor one another (the Church Growth Docent Project™) and by providing the tools for tracking and analyzing a church's leading growth indicators (*DataMirror*™). An

ever-increasing number of churches are partnering with us, asking
God to use these innovative approaches to enlarge the Christian
movement of Jesus Christ.

To receive information on any of these cutting-edge resources,
phone

Charles E. Fuller Institute at 1-800-MAP-META,
fax (1-800-289-6129),

or write

Center for the Development of Leadership for Ministry
P.O. Box 5407
Diamond Bar, CA 91765

Notes

Chapter 1. What Can This Book Do for You?

1. The word *systemic,* used here, accentuates interrelationships and the fact that one part of a system affects the whole. This idea is slightly different from the word *systematic,* which refers to how the system is ordered and organized. I develop this comparison further in the opening paragraphs of chapter 4.

2. C. Peter Wagner, *Your Church Can Grow,* rev. ed. (Ventura, Calif.: Regal, 1984), 111–26.

3. Carl George, *Prepare Your Church for the Future* (Tarrytown, N.Y.: Revell, 1991).

4. Lyle E. Schaller first popularized the concept of ranching that this book will address. He credits the Rev. John F. Anderson, former senior pastor of First Presbyterian Church, Dallas, Texas, with coining the term, which he uses in the following illustration.

Writing on the issue of a minister's leadership style, Schaller compares two images of the role of the pastor. "The more common image is of the shepherd who is directly concerned about and personally involved with each member of the flock. A radically different image is reflected by the comment of the senior minister of a large Presbyterian congregation in Texas: 'When you're the pastor of a congregation as large as this one,' he explained, 'you can't be a shepherd; you have to be a rancher!'" (Lyle E. Schaller, *Survival Tactics in the Parish* [Nashville: Abingdon, 1977], 51.)

In a later book that addresses the church of 450 to 700 in worship attendance, which he calls a ranch, Schaller says: "One of the most important responsibilities of the senior minister is to help the members, and especially the lay leadership, realize this is a ranch and must be operated like a ranch. . . . The primary responsibility of the rancher is to see that larger picture, to operate within a long time frame that is appropriate for a ranch and to resist the pressures (and often the temptation) to plunge in and 'do it myself.' The rancher spends less time 'doing' and more time making sure the job gets done (by someone else) than does the gardener or housekeeper." (Lyle E. Schaller, *Looking in the Mirror: Self-Appraisal in the Local Church,* [Nashville: Abingdon, 1984], 31.) See also Lyle E. Schaller, *Growing Plans: Strategies to Increase Your Church's Membership* (Nashville: Abingdon, 1983), 93–94.

5. Bill M. Sullivan, *Ten Steps to Breaking the 200 Barrier* (Kansas City, Mo.: Beacon Hill Press, 1988), 14.

6. Schaller, *Survival Tactics,* 52–53.

7. Harry H. Fowler, *Breaking Barriers of New Church Growth* (Rocky Mount, N.C.: Creative Growth Dynamics, 129 Gulftide Court, 1988), 55–56.

8. Eddie Gibbs, *I Believe in Church Growth* (Grand Rapids: Eerdmans, 1982), 313, 380–84.

9. Wagner, *Your Church Can Grow,* 52, 77.

See also C. Peter Wagner, writing in the foreword to *A Caring Church,* by Charles A. Ver Straten (Grand Rapids: Baker Book House, 1988).

> Too many churches today expect the ministry of the church to be done by the pastor, not by the people of God. . . . The bulk of the pastoral work of the church can and should be done by lay people. . . .
> On the sheep ranch it is obvious that the only way large numbers of sheep can be adequately cared for is to break them down into smaller bands of sheep assigned to one shepherd. It does not require a degree in organizational management to recognize the wisdom of such structuring. Jethro advised Moses to do it back in the days of the Exodus. . . .
> Research has shown that a chief cause of burnout has been the tendency of pastors falling into the trap of not being able to say *no* to demands on their time. No pastor wants to say no to a church member who is hurting and who needs pastoral care. How . . . can a pastor say *yes* to any and all who need help without entering the burnout syndrome? By delegating the ministry of pastoral care to gifted and trained church members who—believe it or not—can often do a better job at it than the senior pastor could!
> True evangelism brings people to Christ and also into the body of Christ. . . . Unless the members of the body are mobilized to do the ministry of the church, the growth of the church will be limited. At least 80 percent of USA churches are under 200 in attendance. One of the major reasons for this is that the members of those churches unwisely demand that their pastor do all the ministry of the church. A pastor can do all the ministry, but only up to the 200 barrier. If new members are going to be brought into the church and if it is to cross the 200 barrier, it is essential to develop lay shepherding ministries.

Finally, see C. Peter Wagner's *Church Planting for a Greater Harvest* (Ventura, Calif.: Regal, 1990), 113–14:

> The shepherd mode . . . can function well up to the 200 barrier, but not above it. Pastors whose job satisfaction depends heavily on a shepherding ministry are typically small church pastors.
> A rancher mode can take the church through the 200 barrier. The essential difference between the shepherd and the rancher is not whether the sheep are cared for—they are in both cases if things are going as they should. The difference is

who takes care of the sheep. The shepherd must do it personally; the rancher delegates the pastoral care to others.

10. Charles Chaney and Ron Lewis, *Design for Church Growth* (Nashville: Broadman, 1977), 53, 55.

11. Elmer L. Towns, John N. Vaughan, and David J. Seifert, *The Complete Book of Church Growth* (Wheaton: Tyndale House, 1981), 234–37.

Chapter 2. How Can You Enlarge Your Vision?

1. Peter F. Drucker, *The Effective Executive* (New York: Harper & Row, 1985), 113. See also Peter F. Drucker, *Managing the Non-Profit Organization* (New York: HarperCollins, 1990).

2. For further information on clergy salaries, see chapter 10, note 4.

3. Lyle E. Schaller, *Hey, That's Our Church!* (Nashville: Abingdon, 1975). See also Lyle E. Schaller, *Growing Plans: Strategies to Increase Your Church's Membership* (Nashville: Abingdon, 1983), 169; Lyle E. Schaller, *The Small Church Is Different!* (Nashville: Abingdon, 1982), 81; and Dallas Willard, *The Spirit of the Disciplines: Understanding How God Changes Lives* (San Francisco: Harper & Row, 1988).

4. Bill Hybels, *Too Busy Not to Pray: Slowing Down to Be With God* (Downers Grove, Ill.: InterVarsity Press, 1988), 101–6.

Chapter 3. How Does Vision Motivate?

1. Warren Bennis and Burt Nanus, *Leaders: Strategies for Taking Charge* (New York: Harper & Row, 1985).

Also, for an integrated Christian perspective see Merrill J. Oster, *Vision-Driven Leadership* (San Bernardino, Calif.: Here's Life Publishers, 1991).

2. Paul Yonggi Cho with Harold Hostetler, *Successful Home Cell Groups* (Plainfield, N.J.: Logos International, 1981). See also my analysis of Dr. Cho's ministry in *Prepare Your Church for the Future*, 52–53, 134, 213–18.

3. Michael LeBoeuf, *The Greatest Management Principle in the World* (New York: G. P. Putnam's Sons, 1985), 23, 136–37.

4. Loren Cunningham with Janice Rogers, *Is That Really You, God?* (Seattle: YWAM Publishing [P.O. Box 55787, Seattle, WA 98155, 206-771-1153], 1984), 55.

5. North America's first megachurch was First Baptist Church, Fort Worth, Texas, which reported a *Sunday school attendance* of 5,200 in 1928. By 1969 its attendance had significantly declined. A new record was set by Akron Baptist Temple, Akron, Ohio, which reported an average of 5,762 for Sunday school. By 1979 the Sunday school record holder was First Baptist Church, Hammond, Indiana, pastored by Jack Hyles, which reported 15,101 people in average attendance (John N. Vaughan, *The Large Church* [Grand Rapids: Baker Book House, 1985], 12–13, 54–59).

From the late 1970s onward, North America's largest church in *worship atten-dance* was also First Baptist Church, Hammond, Indiana. (Elmer L. Towns, John N. Vaughan, and David J. Seifert, *The Complete Book of Church Growth* [Wheaton: Tyndale House, 1981], 95). During 1992 the top North American atten-dance average for on-campus weekend services was held by either First Baptist Church, Hammond, or Willow Creek Community Church.

In terms of largest worship facilities, the 80,000-square-foot geodesic Faith-Dome, completed in 1989 as the main sanctuary for Crenshaw Christian Center in Los Angeles, has the largest one-room seating capacity (10,140 seats). The founder and present senior pastor of the church is Dr. Frederick K. C. Price.

Elmer L. Towns chronicled large-church growth in the 1960s and 1970s in *America's Fastest Growing Churches* (Nashville: Impact Books, 1973) and in *Christian Life*, September or October editions, 1968–1977. Annual one hundred largest church statistics are compiled by Dr. John N. Vaughan, professor of church growth at Southwest Baptist University and director of the Church Growth Research Center, 1202 E. Austin, Bolivar, MO 65613, (417) 326-1773. His infor-mation has been published in such books as *Almanac of The Christian World 1991–1992,* edited by Edythe Draper (Wheaton: Tyndale House, 1990), 361–63. The second edition, *Almanac of the Christian World 1993–1994,* was published in 1992 and contains the list on pages 361–63.

6. Joel Arthur Barker, *Future Edge: Discovering the New Paradigms of Success* (New York: William Morrow, 1992), 163.

7. Max DePree, *Leadership Is an Art* (New York: Doubleday, 1989), 9. See also George Barna, *The Power of Vision* (Ventura, Calif.: Regal, 1992).

8. See the last section of chapter 9 for an extended explanation of church facili-ties issues.

9. These insights may be found, in expanded form, in *Problem Solving in the Church,* produced by Charles E. Fuller Institute of Evangelism and Church Growth, P.O. Box 90095, Pasadena, CA 91109-5095. Call 1-800-999-9578 or fax 1-800-289-6129.

10. A number of diagnostic tools are available. For the Myers-Briggs approach see Isabel Briggs Myers and Mary H. McCaulley, *Manual: A Guide to the Devel-opment and Use of the Myers-Briggs Type Indicator* (Palo Alto, Calif.: Consulting Psychologists Press, 1985) and David Kiersey and Marilyn Bates, *Please Under-stand Me: Character and Temperament Types* (Del Mar, Calif.: Prometheus, 1984).

The Charles E. Fuller Institute of Evangelism and Church Growth stocks a number of diagnostic tools particularly suitable for churches: various spiritual-gifts inventories, the *Performax Profiles* series (such as the Personal Profile Sys-tem and Biblical Personal Profile System), and the book by Ken Voges and Ron Braund, *Understanding How Others Misunderstand You* (Chicago: Moody, 1990), which explains the DISC format with scriptural illustrations.

Chapter 4. How Would a Church-Growth Consultant Describe Your Church?

1. Cited in Wagner, *Your Church Can Grow,* 47. See McGavran's related discussion in chapter entitled "Methods Which Multiply Churches" in Donald A. McGavran, *How Churches Grow: New Frontiers of Mission* (New York: Friendship Press, 1959), 122–31.

2. ————, *Your Church Can Grow,* 46.

3. George, *Prepare Your Church for the Future,* 26–41.

Chapter 5. Do You Have a Growth Bias?

1. David Johnson and Jeff VanVonderen, *The Subtle Power of Spiritual Abuse: Recognizing and Escaping Spiritual Manipulation and False Spiritual Authority Within the Church* (Minneapolis: Bethany House, 1991), 176.

2. For a catalog of seminar brochures contact the Charles E. Fuller Institute of Evangelism and Church Growth. (See chapter 3, note 9.)

3. See the opening pages of chapter 9 for a more detailed breakdown of typical church sizes.

Chapter 6. Why Develop the Skills of a Rancher?

1. Derek J. Tidball, *Skillful Shepherds: An Introduction to Pastoral Theology* (Grand Rapids: Zondervan/Ministry Resources, 1986), 104–14.

2. Bill Hull, *The Disciple Making Pastor* (Tarrytown, N.Y.: Revell, 1988), 190–202; cf. 74–103, 174–89. See also A. B. Bruce, *The Training of the Twelve,* reprint (Grand Rapids: Kregel, 1971, orig. ed. published 1871). For a biblical theology of equipping, based on a paradigm supportive of a ranching perspective, see Greg Ogden, *The New Reformation: Returning the Ministry to the People of God* (Grand Rapids: Zondervan, 1990), 96–116.

3. For theological analysis of a dependency model, see Ogden, *The New Reformation,* 86–137. For iconoclastic, even sassy, theological analysis, see chapter 7 titled "Luther Went Too Soon" by Gene Edwards and Jim Rutz in *The Open Church,* ed. Jim Rutz (Augusta, Maine: 1992).

4. In my book *Prepare Your Church for the Future,* 42–54, I describe a "zoo" of church sizes from mouse to dinosaur. Each level has special characteristics and requires a different style of leadership.

5. See Elton Trueblood, *The Incendiary Fellowship* (New York: Harper & Row, 1967), 34–54.

Chapter 8. What About "Problem People"?

1. For a different version of the berry bucket theory, which emphasizes how to work with senior formerberries, see chapter 10 of Carl F. George and Robert E.

Logan, *Leading and Managing Your Church: Effective Management for the Christian Professional,* (Tarrytown, N.Y.: Revell, 1987).

2. Lyle E. Schaller, *Activating the Passive Church: Diagnosis and Treatment* (Nashville: Abingdon, 1961), 137–41.

3. Melody Beattie, author of the *New York Times* best-seller *Codependent No More* (San Francisco: Harper/Hazelden, 1987) defines a codependent by quoting recovery pioneer Earnie Larsen: "Those self-defeating learned behaviors or character defects that result in diminished capacity to initiate, or participate in, loving relationships." These and other definitions come from Melody Beattie, *Beyond Codependency: And Getting Better All the Time* (San Francisco: Harper/Hazelden, 1989), 12.

4. Johnson and VanVonderen, *The Subtle Power of Spiritual Abuse,* 68.

5. The Roman Missal, Eucharistic Prayer IV, verses 25–30. For background and commentary see Raymond Maloney, *Our Eucharistic Prayers in Worship, Preaching and Study* (Wilmington, Del.: Michael Glazier, 1985), 66.

6. See "The Hidden Gospel of the 12 Steps," by Tim Stafford. *Christianity Today,* 35:8, July 22, 1991: 14–19; See also "Addicts in the Pew: Interview with Dale Ryan," by Michael G. Maudlin, *Christianity Today,* 35:8, July 22, 1991: 12–21; and *Twelve Steps for Christians* (Recovery Publishing, Inc., 1201 Knoxville St., San Diego, CA 92110–3718, 619-275-1350, 1988).

7. The phrase "not somehow, but triumphantly" comes from the title of a book by missionary-turned-Wheaton-College-president V. Raymond Edman: *Not Somehow, But Triumphantly* (Grand Rapids: Zondervan, 1965).

Chapter 9. How to Break the 200 Barrier

1. The theological foundation for church growth is summarized in C. Peter Wagner, *Strategies for Church Growth: Tools for Effective Mission and Evangelism* (Ventura, Calif.: Regal, 1987), 17–131. More detailed systematic justifications of the Church Growth Movement are in Gibbs, *I Believe in Church Growth;* C. Peter Wagner's *Church Growth and the Whole Gospel: A Biblical Mandate* (New York: Harper & Row, 1981); and Ebbie Smith, *Balanced Church Growth* (Nashville: Broadman, 1984).

2. Some excellent resources that can help the smaller church begin to experience a growth momentum are: C. Wayne Zunkel, *Growing the Small Church: A Guide for Church Members* (Elgin, Ill.: David C. Cook, 1983), Zunkel, *Growing the Small Church: A Guide for Church Leaders* (Elgin, Ill.: David C. Cook, 1982); Carl S. Dudley, *Making the Small Church Effective* (Nashville: Abingdon, 1978); Carl S. Dudley and Douglas Alan Walrath, *Developing Your Small Church's Potential* (Valley Forge, Pa.: Judson Press, 1988); Harry H. Fowler, *Breaking Barriers on New Church Growth* (Rocky Mount, N.C.: Creative Growth Dynamics, 1988); Sullivan, *Ten Steps to Breaking the 200 Barrier;* Lyle E. Schaller, *Forty-Four Ways to Increase Church Attendance* (Nashville: Abingdon, 1988).

3. This is Lyle E. Schaller's observation as well in *Activating the Passive Church: Diagnosis and Treatment* (Nashville: Abingdon, 1981), 25–26, and *Growing Plans,* 11.

4. Church consultants use a number of tools for keeping score: average worship attendance of adults only, average worship attendance of adults and children, peak worship attendance (i.e., Easter or Christmas Eve), Sunday school average attendance, Sunday school membership, baptized membership, confirmed membership, total membership, and resident membership, just to name a few.

This book focuses on average worship attendance of adults and children (total nose count) because this particular tally offers one of the most accurate barometers, both predictive and descriptive, of church personality, style, and sociological characteristics.

See also the comment on comparing membership to attendance in footnote 7 of this chapter.

5. This number is commonly cited in church growth literature. There are various ways the 400,000 figure is calculated. For example, *Yearbook of American and Canadian Churches, 1992,* edited by Kenneth B. Bedell and Alice M. Jones (Nashville: Abingdon, 1992), 265–77, gives a denomination-by-denomination breakdown. George Barna, *The Frog in the Kettle* (Ventura, Calif.: Regal, 1990), 130, uses a different formula to reach approximately the same total.

6. Lyle E. Schaller, noting that one fourth of all North American Protestant churches average fewer than 35 at worship and that at least one half average less than 75, concludes, "the normative size for a Protestant congregation in the North American culture probably varies between 20 and 60 at the principal weekly worship service. One third of all Protestant congregations [in North America] fit into this bracket." *Growing Plans,* 18. See also Schaller, *The Multiple Staff and the Larger Church* (Nashville: Abington,1980), 28; William C. Tinsley, *Upon This Rock* (Nashville: Abingdon, 1980), 9. His figures include both adults and children.

The specific examples in this chapter's charts update and confirm the accuracy of the data, but also illustrate the wide variance between denominations.

7. Size statistics are based on 1991 data from a cross section of denominations (large and small; mainline, evangelical, and charismatic; etc.). Other researchers have reached similar conclusions and made various observations from the data. See, for example, Lyle E. Schaller, *The Small Church Is Different* (Nashville: Abingdon, 1982), 58; Lyle E. Schaller, *The Multiple Staff and the Larger Church* (Nashville: Abingdon, 1980), 28; William C. Tinsley, *Upon This Rock* (Nashville: Southern Baptist Home Mission Board, 1985), 80–87.

The number of churches with a worship attendance of 1,000 or more varies widely according to denomination: one of every 600 (United Methodist), one of every 400 (Nazarene), one of every 300 (all Lutherans and Presbyterians combined), one of every 250 (American Baptist), one of every 200 (Southern Baptist), and one of every 100 (Assemblies of God). See Lyle E. Schaller, "Megachurch!" *Christianity Today,* 34:4, March 5, 1990:20.

Using *membership* as a guideline, a Gallup Organization poll reported in the
Statistical Abstract of the United States, 110th ed. (Washington, D.C.: U.S.
Department of Commerce, 1991), 57, indicates that, of denominational churches in
the continental United States:

21% have fewer than 100 members

19% have 100–199 members

14% have 200–299 members

11% have 300–399 members

7% have 400–499 members

16% have 500–999 members

7% have 1,000–2,000 members

5% have 2,000 or more members

It is extremely difficult, however, to correlate membership with attendance. In
some churches, particularly those in the holiness traditions, attendance may be
higher than membership. In others, particularly long-established mainline
churches, membership may be two to five times higher than attendance.

8. See chapter 3, note 5 on annual one hundred largest churches statistics.

9. C. Peter Wagner, *Church Planting for a Greater Harvest* (Ventura, Calif.:
Regal, 1990), 130.

10. Ibid., 131. One of the first writers to develop this concept was Carl Dudley,
Making the Small Church Effective, 32–35.

11. Quoted by Russell Chandler in *Racing Toward 2001: The Forces Shaping
America's Religious Future* (Grand Rapids: Zondervan, 1992), 292. Emphasis is
Mr. Chandler's.

12. Elmer Towns, *Ten of Today's Most Innovative Churches: What They're
Doing, How They're Doing It and How You Can Apply Their Ideas in Your Church*
(Ventura, Calif.: Regal, 1990), 243.

13. For details and examples see my book, *Prepare Your Church for the
Future,* especially pages 122–29.

Chapter 10. How to Break the 400 Barrier

1. See chapter 8 for a discussion of ministers' dysfunctional households. For an
application of family-systems insights to church staff relationships, see Anne
Marie Nuechterlein, *Improving Your Multiple Staff Ministry: How to Work
Together More Effectively* (Minneapolis: Augsburg, 1989).

2. See chapter 8, note 3, for a definition of codependency.

3. Lyle E. Schaller, *Parish Planning* (Nashville: Abingdon, 1971), 38–46, 63.
See also Lyle E. Schaller and Charles A. Tidwell, *Creative Church Administration*
(Nashville: Abingdon, 1975), 45–54, 62–65; Lyle E. Schaller, *Forty-Four Ways to
Revitalize the Women's Organization* (Nashville: Abingdon, 1990), 76–77; Lyle E.

Schaller, *Create Your Own Future: Alternatives for the Long-Range Planning Committee* (Nashville, Abingdon, 1991), 26, 59.

4. For salary surveys contact Christian Management Association, P. O. Box 4638, Diamond Bar, CA 91765, 714-861-8861 (115 positions listed in a 300-page book); National Association of Church Business Administrators, 7001 Grapevine Hwy., Suite 324, Fort Worth, TX 76180-8813, 817-284-1732 (25 personnel positions, rated by church size, 370 pages); Christianity Today, Inc., 465 Gundersen Drive, Carol Stream, IL 60188, 800-722-7744 (24 positions, rated by church size). Also many denominations publish how-to-determine-compensation type books.

5. See Kenneth K. Kilinhski and Jerry C. Wofford, *Organization and Leadership in the Local Church* (Grand Rapids: Zondervan, 1973), 174. See also Charles E. Tidwell, *Church Administration—Effective Leadership for Ministry* (Nashville: Broadman, 1985, rev. 1991), 114–15.

6. I discuss the development of contemporary staffing patterns according to church size in my book, *Prepare Your Church for the Future,* 42–54.

7. Drucker's emphasis on working from strength is highlighted in "Managing to Minister: An Interview with Peter Drucker," *Leadership,* X:2, Spring 1989:18. His definition of good management comes from *The Effective Executive* (New York: Harper & Row, 1985), 71, where he says: "To make strength productive is the unique purpose of organization. It cannot, of course, overcome the weaknesses with which each of us is abundantly endowed. But it can make them irrelevant."

8. For a biblical and church-oriented perspective on delegation see *Leading and Managing Your Church,* by Carl F. George and Robert E. Logan (Tarrytown, N.Y.: Revell, 1987), especially chapter 7, "Developing People through Delegation." Also: Myron Rush, *Management: A Biblical Approach* (Wheaton: Victor Books, 1983), Stephen Douglas, et al., *The Ministry of Management* (San Bernardino, Calif.: Here's Life, 1981).

9. Larry D. Baker, "Delegating Effectively for Better Results," in chapter 13 of *The Management Team* ed. Dorothy M. Walters (Glendora, Calif.: Royal Cassettes, Books, and Speakers, Inc., 1984), 211.

10. The idea for these examples came from Orville E. Easterly, "How Delegated Work Boomerangs," 40–41.

Chapter 11. How to Break the 800 Barrier

1. I explain these concepts in far greater detail in *Prepare Your Church for the Future,* chapter 9, 119–49. See also Charles Tidwell, *Church Administration,* 106–7.

2. A good starting point is two books by George Barna, *Marketing the Church: What They Never Taught You about Church Growth* (Colorado Springs: NavPress, 1988) and *Church Marketing: Breaking Ground for the Harvest* (Ventura, Calif.: Regal, 1992). Other solid tools are Norman Shawchuck, Philip Kotler, Bruce Wrenn, and Gustave Rath, *Marketing for Congregations: Choosing to Serve People More Effectively* (Nashville: Abingdon, 1992); Robert Bask, *Attracting*

New Members (New York: Reformed Church of America, 1988); and a secular title, Carl Sewell, *Customers for Life* (New York: Doubleday, 1990).

3. *Prepare Your Church for the Future,* 42–54.

4. Schaller, "Megachurch!", 20.

5. See the references to lists of one hundred largest churches in chapter 3, note 5, and accompanying discussion in the text of the chapter.

6. Lyle E. Schaller, *The Seven-Day-A-Week Church* (Nashville: Abingdon, 1992), 28.

7. _____, 149.

8. _____, *Choices for Churches,* 87.

9. John N. Vaughan, "Characteristics of Growing Churches," *Growing Churches,* Sunday School Board of the Southern Baptist Convention, 1:2, Jan–March 1991: 16.

10. John N. Vaughan, "Megamyths," *Christianity Today,* 34:4 March 5, 1990:24.

11. Lyle E. Schaller, *Forty-Four Ways to Increase Church Attendance* (Nashville: Abingdon, 1988), 89. See also pp. 12, 39, 45. See also Schaller, *Growing Plans,* 116; Schaller, *The Senior Minister* (Nashville: Abingdon, 1988), 110–14; Schaller, *The Seven-Day-A-Week Church,* 106; and Schaller, *Looking in the Mirror: Self-Appraisal in the Local Church* (Nashville: Abingdon, 1984), 150.

Chapter 12. How to Break the Care Barrier

1. Russell Chandler, *Racing Toward 2001: The Forces Shaping America's Religious Future* (Grand Rapids: Zondervan, 1992), 164.

2. George Barna, *What Americans Believe (*Ventura, Calif.: Regal, 1991), 234–37.

3. _____, *The Frog in the Kettle,* 137. Italics not in the original.

4. George Gallup, "The Unchurched American—Ten Years Later" (Princeton, N.J.: The Princeton Religion Research Center, 1988), cited in "To Verify . . ." *Leadership,* Winter 1989:81.

5. This 80 percent figure is a rounded figure commonly cited by church growth researchers. For example, separate quotations from Win Arn, Kirk Hadaway, and Robert Dale are cited in *Reviving the Plateaued Church* by R. D. Baker, Truman Brown, Jr., and Robert D. Dale (Nashville: Convention Press, 1992), 7. Even strongly evangelistic denominations report that most of their churches are not experiencing growth. For example, Southern Baptists found that between 1985 and 1990, only 30.2 percent of their churches grew, whereas 51 percent were plateaued and 18.8 percent declined. A plateau is "based on a membership change of plus or minus 10 percent during a five-year period," and a decline is "based on membership losses of over 10 percent during a five-year period." (Linda S. Barr, ed., *Southern Baptist Handbook 1991* [Nashville: Sunday School Board of the Southern Baptist Convention, 1991], 18, 141).

6. George Barna, *What Americans Believe* (Ventura, Calif.: Regal, 1991), 234.

7. In *Filling the Holes in Our Souls* (Chicago: Moody, 1992) coauthors Paul Meier, Gene A. Getz, Richard A. Meier, and Allen R. Doran describe the "small group revolution" as "what may be the most significant phenomenon in the Christian church in the late twentieth century" (20).

8. John N. Vaughan has documented the sizes of the world's largest churches. He describes them in a video series entitled *Megachurches of the World* (Church Growth Research Center, 1202 E. Austin, Bolivar, MO 65613, 417-326-1773) and in his book, *The World's Twenty Largest Churches* (Grand Rapids: Baker Book House, 1984). I summarize them in my book, *Prepare Your Church for the Future,* 50–51. Ralph Neighbour, Jr., comments on several of them in *Where Do We Go From Here?* (Houston: Touch Publications [P.O. Box 19888, Houston, TX 77224, 1-800-735-5865], 1990).

9. Perhaps the most visible model of the lay-pastor-led cell-model church in North America is New Hope Community Church, Portland, Oregon. Planted in 1972, it is now the twenty-seventh largest in the United States. The founding pastor, Dale E. Galloway, summarizes its philosophy and ministry in *20/20 Vision: How to Create a Successful Church with Lay Pastors and Cell Groups* (Portland, Oreg.: Scott Publishing Company [11731 S.E. Stevens Road, Portland, OR 97266, 503-659-5683], 1986).

10. Cited in "To Verify . . .," *Leadership Journal,* 12:2, Spring 1991:114, and taken from *American Demographics,* 12:11, November 1990. Schaller poses the question, Are there too many churches? and gives a statistical rationale for answering in *The Small Church Is Different!* (Nashville: Abingdon, 1982), 126–29.

11. Contact Stephen Ministries, 8016 Dale Ave., St. Louis, MO 63117, phone 314-645-5511, fax 314-645-9133.

12. See George, *Prepare Your Church for the Future,* 31–33.

13. "Church Growth Fine Tunes Its Formulas," *Christianity Today,* 35:7, June 24, 1991: 47.

14. Paul Yonggi Cho, writing in the "Foreword" to John N. Vaughan's *The Large Church: A Twentieth-Century Expression of the First-Century Church* (Grand Rapids: Baker Book House, 1985), 9.

15. Cho and Hostetler, *Successful Home Cell Groups,* 64.

16. "Church Growth," *Christianity Today,* 47.

17. *Time,* June 1, 1992:54, citing the United Nations Population Fund.

18. George, *Prepare Your Church for the Future,* 20.

19. See, for example, Nathan Keyfitz, *Applied Mathematical Demography,* second ed. (New York: Springer-Verlag, 1985), 1–14.

20. See the statistics from Ralph D. Winter, U.S. Center for World Mission, 1605 Elizabeth Street, Pasadena, CA 91104, as summarized in such publications as *Mission Frontiers,* January–February 1992:5.

Bibliography

Arn, Win, and Charles Arn. *The Master's Plan for Making Disciples.* Pasadena, Calif.: Church Growth Press (1921 S. Myrtle Ave., Monrovia, CA 91016, 818-305-1280), 1982, 176 pages.

Develops the *oikos* evangelism principle of identifying people movements which travel along natural webs of relationship.

Arnold, Jeffrey. *The Big Book on Small Groups.* Downers Grove, Ill.: InterVarsity, 1990, 264 pages.

Building a strong small group requires time, energy, and skill. The author discusses such sticky issues as how to communicate and maintain group goals, how to develop relationships within the group, how to train small group leaders, and how to implement a small group outreach program.

Barker, Joel Arthur. *Future Edge: Discovering the New Paradigms of Success.* New York: William Morrow, 1992, 240 pages.

A secular writer makes a compelling case for the role of paradigms in interpreting the experience and success of an organization. Pastors and lay leaders will have no trouble using the paradigm concept to apply problem solving to the church.

Barna, George. *Church Marketing: Breaking Ground for the Harvest.* Ventura, Calif.: Regal, 1992, 250 pages.

The author helps readers create a marketing plan, shows how to design and conduct congregational and community surveys, and explains techniques for using the mass media for ministry value.

Barna, George. *The Power of Vision: How You Can Capture and Apply God's Vision for Your Ministry.* Ventura, Calif.: Regal, 1992, 192 pages.

Highlights such topics as how vision is different from mission, why a mission statement is not the same thing as vision, and practical steps to take in discovering and implementing God's unique vision for your ministry.

213

Barna, George. *What Americans Believe.* Ventura, Calif.: Regal, 1991, 306 pages.

This exhaustive resource is the distillation of a major survey. It provides a snapshot of 65 values, lifestyles, beliefs, and mores of the "typical" American.

Bennis, Warren, and Burt Nanus. *Leaders: The Strategies for Taking Charge.* New York: Harper & Row, 1985, 244 pages.

Pivotal for understanding the distinction between being a leader, such as the senior pastor as primary vision caster, and a manager, such as a staff pastor who answers the how-to questions.

Biehl, Bobb, and Ted Engstrom. *Increasing Your Boardroom Confidence.* Sisters, Oreg.: Questar, 1988, 288 pages.

"The best place to begin" for church leaders in need of a master plan, according to *Leadership* magazine (Spring 1989 issue). The step-by-step approach includes "30 Questions to Ask Yourself before Making Major Decisions" and "The Recruitment Process."

Bryson, O. J. *Networking the Kingdom.* Waco: Word, 1990, 233 pages.

Based on seven-member teams, Bryson's strategy systematically penetrates a community by utilizing the greatest asset of any church—its people. His concept answers how to reclaim former churchgoers in an easy, natural, and productive way.

Chandler, Russell. *Racing Toward 2001: The Forces Shaping America's Religious Future.* Grand Rapids: Zondervan, 1992, 367 pages.

An award-winning journalist looks at the power of the Christian faith in light of the changes in technology, lifestyle, and family makeup. He proposes ways that churches can both deflect and direct these massive changes.

Chaney, Charles, and Ron Lewis. *Design for Church Growth.* Nashville: Broadman, 1977, 216 pages.

A practical guide for pastors and other church leaders. This book explains how growth is not an accident; it's something to be planned and worked for. Tools, step-by-step guidance.

Cho, Paul Yonggi, with Harold Hostetler. *Successful Home Cell Groups.* Plainfield, N.J.: Logos International, 1981, 176 pages.

The founding pastor of the largest church in the history of Christendom introduces his story with these words: "Church growth is only a by-product. The real secret is home cell groups. . . ." This fascinating narrative is not so much a how-to book as a glimpse into the soul of Dr. Cho and the cell-group ministry he developed.

Clinton, J. Robert. *The Making of a Leader.* Colorado Springs: NavPress, 1988, 272 pages.

By studying the lives of hundreds of historical, biblical, and contemporary leaders, the author, a professor at Fuller Theological Seminary School of World Mission, has determined six stages of leadership development. He offers checkpoints to clarify where you are in the process.

Coleman, Lyman. *Serendipity Small Group Training Manual.* Littleton, Colo.: Serendipity House, 1991, 96 pages.

Creative, realistic game plan for training the leadership of a small group. Covers everything from why a church needs small groups, to common problems and solutions, to case study profiles.

Dale, Robert D. *Ministers As Leaders.* Nashville: Broadman, 1984, 132 pages.

Addresses different leadership styles: what they are, their origin, and their effects on others. Proposes that leaders be more interactive.

————. *To Dream Again.* Nashville: Broadman, 1981, 160 pages.

This resource targets plateaued churches, helping them analyze their patterns and move back into a pattern of growth.

Dayton, Edward R., and Ted W. Engstrom. *Strategy for Leadership.* Tarrytown, N.Y.: Revell, 1979, 240 pages.

This book summarizes the accumulated experience of these effective leaders. It highlights principles at work in the business world, parachurch organizations, and churches.

Dudley, Carl S. *Making the Small Church Effective.* Nashville: Abingdon, 1978, 180 pages.

A well-written apology for small churches and their integrity. Not growth oriented.

Dudley, Carl S., and Douglas Alan Walrath. *Developing Your Small Church's Potential.* Valley Forge, Pa.: Judson, 1988, 96 pages.

The authors explain how to make positive use of community transition, absorb newcomers into a church family, reshape a church image, resolve cultural conflicts, develop programs reflecting the community's; needs, and use the past as a bridge to the future.

Engstrom, Ted, with Norman B. Rohrer. *The Art of Mentoring: Passing on to Others What God Has Given You.* Brentwood, Tenn.: Wolgemuth & Hyatt, 1990, 192 pages.

Sage advice from the former president of one of the largest parachurch agencies (World Vision) in North America. The book excels both in management advice and in a passion for excellence. Includes sections on why mentoring is the best way to learn and on how to choose a mentor.

Exman, Gary W. *Get Ready . . . Get Set . . . Grow! Church Growth for Town and Country Congregations.* Lima, Ohio: CSS Publishing Co., (628 South Main Street, Lima, OH 45804, 419-227-1818), 1987, 148 pages.

Written from a Methodist perspective, this book offers practical insights, tools, and encouragement for pastors of smaller churches, whatever their denominational background.

Fowler, Harry H. *Breaking Barriers of New Church Growth.* Rocky Mount, N.C.: Creative Growth Dynamics (129 Gulftide Court, Rocky Mount, N.C. 27801), 1988, 127 pages.

Case studies of Southern Baptist churches which have gone through what the author perceives as the 35 barrier, the 75 barrier, and the 125 barrier. Offers principles relevant to each stage.

Galloway, Dale E. *20/20 Vision: How to Create a Successful Church with Lay Pastors and Cell Groups.* Portland, Oreg.: Scott Publishing Company (11731 S.E. Stevens Road, Portland, OR 97266, 503-659-5683), 1986, 160 pages.

The primary case study that churches emulate when they want to provide maximum pastoral care for their people. Galloway presents a comprehensive and practical treatment of the cell-group principles used to build the 6,000-person New Hope Community Church in Portland, Oregon.

_____. *Lay Pastor Training Manual for Successful Home Group Meetings.* Portland, Oreg.: New Hope Community Church, 1986, 47 pages.

This companion to the book *20/20 Vision* describes the day-to-day responsibilities of being a lay pastor. Used by hundreds of churches to train cell leaders and apprentices, it offers leadership tips, job descriptions, accountability forms, and other practical helps for beginning and maintaining home group meetings.

George, Carl F. *Prepare Your Church for the Future.* Tarrytown, N.Y.: Revell, 1991, 240 pages.

Foundational for anyone investigating the Meta-Church paradigm. It paints a broad picture of what a cell-group driven church looks like, including insights on how celebration and cell interrelate. As it urges and inspires pastors to place a higher priority on the formation of lay leaders, it offers a specific infrastructure and a leadership-training model for doing so.

George, Carl F., and Robert E. Logan. *Leading and Managing Your Church.* Tarrytown, N.Y.: Revell, 1987, 192 pages.

How to build an effective ministry team? How to translate vision into reachable goals? How to obtain widespread goal ownership? This book contains workable answers from authors who effectively blend biblical principles, sound management insights and ministry-based practical experiences.

Getz, Gene A. *Building Up One Another.* Wheaton: Scripture, 1978, 120 pages.

How every member of the church can help strengthen fellow Christians.

Gibbs, Eddie. *I Believe in Church Growth.* London: Hodder & Stoughton, 1985 (rev. ed.), 312 pages.

The author, a church growth professor at Fuller Theological Seminary, combines sound scholarship with a readable style. Many of his examples come from his native Anglican church in England.

Griffin, Em. *Getting Together.* Downers Grove, Ill.: InterVarsity, 1982, 233 pages.

The author describes three kinds of groups—talk, relationship, and influence—and explores their dynamics.

Hadaway, C. Kirk, Stuart A. Wright, and Francis M. Dubose. *Home Cell Groups and House Churches: Alternatives for the Urban Church.* Nashville: Broadman, 1987, 264 pages.

Explores the home cell group and house church movement in a scholarly but readable fashion. Shows how to incorporate this movement into the local church.

Hamlin, Judy. *Curriculum and Small Group Resource Guide.* Colorado Springs: NavPress, 1991, 287 pages.

A catalog of virtually every small-group curriculum resource published in America, including study guides, books with leaders, guides, video resources, and youth group curriculum.

_____. *The Small Group Leader's Training Course.* Colorado Springs: NavPress, 1990, 207 pages.

This course contains the tools needed to help your leaders develop and refine the skills that will give them maximum effectiveness in ministry. Designed to provide a balance of instruction and hands-on experience.

Handy, Charles. *The Age of Unreason.* Boston: Harvard Business School Press, 1989, 278 pages.

Today's organizations must confront constant developments in technology. Handy demonstrates that what has worked in the past may no longer do so. He provides an incisive look at the kinds of organizations that will thrive in the future.

Hassinger, Edward W., John S. Holik, and J. Kenneth Benson. *The Rural Church.* Nashville: Abingdon, 1988, 169 pages.

A highly informative study of churches in communities of under 2,500 showing changes over three decades. Lyle Schaller's foreword is excellent.

Haugk, Kenneth C. *Antagonists in the Church: How to Identify and Deal with Destructive Conflict.* Minneapolis: Augsburg, 1988, 189 pages.

Although only a very few people are antagonists, these individuals have the potential to disrupt and even destroy a church's mission and ministry. The author, a clinical psychologist who founded the Stephen Series system of lay caring, offers fresh insight and practical tools for coping with antagonism when it arises.

Hunter, George G., III. *The Contagious Congregation.* Nashville: Abingdon, 1979, 150 pages.

Hunter, the top evangelism executive for the United Methodist Church, immersed himself in church-growth studies at Fuller Theological Seminary before taking up his assignment in Nashville in 1977. This book contains fresh insights into the growth of established churches.

Hunter, Kent R. *Foundations for Church Growth.* New Haven, Mo.: Leader, 1983, 204 pages.

One of the best introductions to church-growth principles. This is written from a Lutheran point of view but the ideas are practical for all.

_____. *Your Church Has Personality.* Nashville: Abingdon, 1985, 120 pages.

A ground-breaking book which lays out the meaning of philosophy of ministry. Kent Hunter, a leading church-growth consultant, draws on wide experience to produce this practical guidebook, which will help any pastor who uses it. He includes biblical and theological foundations, role models, and how-to sections for writing your church's philosophy of ministry.

Johnson, David, and Jeff VanVonderen. *The Subtle Power of Spiritual Abuse.* Minneapolis: Bethany House, 1991, 235 pages.

The book describes situations where seemingly spiritual means are used by authority figures in an attempt to meet their own needs of importance, power, intimacy, or spiritual gratification. Shows how to identify destructive and abusive dynamics within a church.

Jones, E. Stanley. *Conversion.* Nashville: Abingdon, 1946, reprinted and updated, 1991, 256 pages.

A world-famous author and missionary sheds light on the joy, peace, and satisfaction that comes with conversion, including insights into what conversion is, how it comes about, and its lasting effects for the convert.

Keirsey, David and Marilyn Bates. *Please Understand Me: Character and Temperament Types.* Del Mar, Calif.: Prometheus Nemesis, 1984, 210 pages.

A scholarly but very readable introduction to the Myers-Briggs Type Indicator.

Kraft, Charles H. *Christianity With Power.* Ann Arbor, Mich.: Servant, 1989, 230 pages.

The author, a former missionary and now professor of anthropology at Fuller Theological Seminary, believes many modern Christians have become embarrassed and reluctant to preach a gospel accompanied by supernatural power. He urges a return to the biblical paradigm that accepts signs and wonders as instruments of God.

Larson, Knute. *Growing Adults on Sunday Morning: Nurturing Community through Adult Bible Fellowships.* Wheaton: Victor, 1991, 119 pages.

Proposes adult Bible fellowships (ABFs) as a step beyond traditional adult Sunday school. Contains many valuable suggestions for improving the care quality of congregation-sized groups, although many of these needs could be met better by small cell groups.

Lavin, Ronald J. *You Can Grow in a Small Group.* Lima, Ohio: C.S.S. Publishing Co. (628 South Main Street, Lima, OH 45804, 419-227-1818), 1976, 139 pages.

Tells a powerful story of a family who made it through the trauma of a medical crisis because of the koinonia of a small group. Describes how to set up such a small-group program. The author is a Lutheran pastor.

Logan, Robert E. *Beyond Church Growth.* Tarrytown, N.Y.: Revell, 1989, 220 pages.

This practical, biblically based strategy for stimulating effective lay ministry highlights these elements of Meta-Church technology: visionized faith, celebrative worship, VHS for developing and coaching lay leaders, ever expanding networks of cell groups, and laity mobilized by spiritual gifts.

Malphurs, Aubrey. *Developing a Vision for Ministry in the 21st Century.* Grand Rapids: Baker Book House, 1992.

"Strong leaders possess a vision as great as God and as specific as a zip code," says the foreword to this book. The author, a professor at Dallas Theological Seminary, offers six specific steps for birthing, developing, and casting vision.

Maner, Robert E. *Making the Small Church Grow.* Kansas City, Mo.: Beacon Hill, 1982, 100 pages.

Maner is a Nazarene pastor who has served small churches and tells what God has done to make them grow.

May, Gerald G. *Addiction and Grace.* San Francisco: Harper & Row, 1988, 192 pages.

A Christian psychiatrist describes the roots of addiction, explaining how it affects the mind, body, and spirit. Then he shows how prayer, grace, and the wisdom of spiritual traditions can help overcome it.

McBride, Neil F. *How to Lead Small Groups.* Colorado Springs: NavPress, 1990, 141 pages.

The author guides a leader through the critical aspects of providing solid leadership to a Bible study or other small group.

McGavran, Donald A. *Understanding Church Growth* (rev. ed.). Grand Rapids: William B. Eerdmans, 1980, 450 pages.

This classic textbook by the father of the church growth movement is the best starting point for any serious student of the field.

McGavran, Donald, and Win Arn. *How to Grow a Church.* Ventura, Calif.: Regal, 1973, 180 pages.

Cast in a question-and-answer format, this top-seller summarizes the views of two leaders in the church growth movement.

McGavran, Donald, and George G. Hunter, III. *Church Growth: Strategies That Work.* Nashville: Abingdon, 1980, 120 pages.

One of the best primers on the church growth movement, this book also provides practical tips on motivating people for growth, training laity, helping small churches grow, and planting new churches.

McGinnis, Alan Loy. *Bringing out the Best in People.* Minneapolis: Augsburg, 1985, 191 pages.

The author of *The Friendship Factor* offers twelve practical principles of how to motivate others to excellence. An excellent tool for coaching leaders of various task-and-nurture groups.

Mavis, W. Curry. *Advancing the Smaller Church.* Grand Rapids: Baker, 1968, 180 pages.

A good, growth-focused book designed to help the small church get on its feet and grow.

Mitchell, Kenneth R. *Multiple Staff Ministries.* Philadelphia: Westminster, 1988, 164 pages.

Mitchell, an experienced family therapist and pastoral counselor, suggests that staff tensions can be understood if the particular staff system is analyzed. He discusses the roles, rules, and rituals that keep a staff team together.

Murren, Doug. *The Baby Boomerang.* Ventura, Calif.: Regal, 1990, 287 pages.

The author, who pastors a church of baby boomers, shows keen insight into how boomers think, behave, and believe. He offers more than hope; he presents a road map to the hearts and souls of the boomer generation.

Neighbour, Ralph W. *Where Do We Go From Here?* Houston: Touch Publications (P.O. Box 19888, Houston, TX 77224, 1-800-735-5865), 1990, 463 pages.

A passionate, theologically rooted appeal to build churches on the cell-church model. The author, who comes from a strongly programmatic background, offers case studies of huge cell churches around the world. His examples provide the reader with many how-to ideas and equipping tools.

Nicholas, Ron, ed. *Small Group Leader's Handbook.* Downers Grove, Ill.: Inter-Varsity, 1982, 194 pages.

This collection of articles focuses on the specialized training skill sets needed to conduct vibrant small groups.

Nuechterlein, Anne Marie. *Improving Your Multiple Staff Ministry: How to Work Together More Effectively,* Minneapolis: Augsburg, 1989, 160 pages.

The author offers helpful insight into a number of factors present in any church staff; a variety of expectations, preferences, personality types, levels of self-esteem, power, and ability to communicate.

Ogden, Greg. *The New Reformation: Returning the Ministry to the People of God.* Grand Rapids: Zondervan, 1990, 224 pages.

This book offers a unique understanding of the vital dynamics of leadership and ministry by laity. It details both the theology and practice of lay ministry.

Ott, E. Stanley. *The Vibrant Church.* Ventura, Calif.: Regal, 1989, 249 pages.

This Presbyterian pastor lays the foundation for creating person-to-person ministries and discipleship communities in a church. He offers a fresh look at the theology and practice of people-building ministry.

Peace, Richard. *Small Group Evangelism.* Downers Grove, Ill.: InterVarsity, 1985, 190 pages.

This book presents basic principles and then outlines a nine-to-thirteen-week training program.

Rothauge, Arlin J. *Sizing Up a Congregation for New Member Ministry.* New York: Episcopal Church Center, 1983, 38 pages.

The author assumes that any size church can attract and assimilate new members, but that the most effective means will vary with the size of the congregation. Thus he offers a strategy for each of four sizes.

Schaef, Anne Wilson. *When Society Becomes an Addict.* San Francisco: Harper & Row, 1987, 192 pages.

An incisive look at the system of addiction pervasive in Western society today.

Schaller, Lyle E. *Activating the Passive Church: Diagnosis and Treatment.* Nashville: Abingdon, 1961, 159 pages.

This book diagnoses the causes of church passivity, and formulates a method for combating the problem. It also shows how to overcome loss of direction in a church.

———. *The Change Agent.* Nashville: Abingdon, 1972.

The author maps out a number of strategies that address the difficulties, processes, and results of change. Helpful insights for the inevitable tough times when a church, especially a long-established one, faces the challenge of innovation.

———. *Forty-Four Questions for Church Planters.* Nashville: Abingdon, 1992, 192 pages.

This is Schaller's first book specifically on church planting. He offers judicious advice on the demanding questions that church planters raise.

———. *Forty-Four Steps Up Off the Plateau.* Nashville: Abingdon, 1992, 180 pages.

Schaller defines a plateau as a stagnant holding point in the size and energy of a church—a level at which energy is focused entirely on maintenance of existing structures. He outlines forty-four steps needed to break the bonds that tie down such a church.

———. *Growing Plans: Strategies to Increase Your Church's Membership.* Nashville: Abingdon, 1983, 176 pages.

Effectively using an informative case-history approach to outline church-growth strategies, Schaller proposes that visitation evangelism is the ideal method of obtaining new members. He then outlines four other strategies for increasing the size of a church.

———. *It's a Different World: The Challenge for Today's Pastor.* Nashville: Abingdon, 1987, 239 pages.

This book helps church leaders understand and effectively grapple with the "new realities" of church life today, including the reason for the decline of mainline churches, the feminization of society, and the demise of the traditional family and community.

———. *Looking in the Mirror: Self-Appraisal in the Local Church.* Nashville: Abingdon, 1984, 206 pages.

"Frequently," says this veteran church consultant, "it's difficult or impossible for congregational leaders to agree on the role God is calling the church to fill unless they can agree on contemporary reality." This book provides a conceptual framework necessary for a church to self-appraise its ministry.

————. *The Middle Sized Church.* Nashville: Abingdon, 1985, 160 pages.

This is a companion volume to his books on the smaller church and the larger church. Schaller examines the personality and unique opportunities facing the church of several hundred, with particular attention to the denominational and long-established church.

————. *The Multiple Staff and the Larger Church.* Nashville: Abingdon, 1980, 142 pages.

Large churches are different in expectations, performance, staffing, and use of lay volunteers. Schaller fully describes the differences that mark the larger church and offers much specific advice to this specialized group.

————. *The Seven-Day-a-Week Church.* Nashville: Abingdon, 1992, 192 pages.

With brilliant insight and engaging description, Schaller reveals the reasons behind the worldwide emergence of megachurches. He describes characteristics of both the church and the kind of person who pastors it.

————. *The Small Church* Is *Different.* Nashville: Abingdon, 1982, 192 pages.

With characteristic insight and clarity, Schaller has authored probably the most helpful book on understanding small churches yet published. It is value free as to whether or not small churches should grow.

————. *Survival Tactics in the Parish.* Nashville: Abingdon, 1977, 208 pages.

Schaller applies his trouble-shooting experience and skills to a host of sticky questions, including, Who was my predecessor? How do I follow a long-term pastorate? and What does my congregation expect?

Schaller, Lyle E., and Charles A. Tidwell. *Creative Church Administration.* Nashville: Abingdon, 1975, 208 pages.

Two top church consultants give practical advice on numerous issues, including motivation, volunteer leaders, and financial planning.

Smalley, Gary, and John Trent. *The Blessing.* Nashville: Thomas Nelson, 1986, 224 pages.

The authors suggest that many Christians spend much of their lives, without even realizing it, striving for approval from family members. The book includes counseling insights on how to insure that children, husbands, and wives feel security and family approval.

Smedes, Lewis B. *Caring and Commitment: Learning to Live the Love We Promise.* San Francisco: Harper & Row, 1988, 176 pages.

Presents guidelines for considering and making solid commitments that support the keeping of faith with one another and with oneself.

Synder, Howard A. *The Community of the King.* Downers Grove, Ill.: InterVarsity, 1977, 216 pages.

The author believes that gifts, more than offices, should guide the church's operation. He probes the relationship between the kingdom of God and the church as we know it in our daily lives.

Snyder, Howard A. *The Problem with Wineskins.* Downers Grove, Ill.: InterVarsity, 1975, 214 pages.

What kinds of church structures are most compatible with the gospel in modern society? The author's goal in tackling this question is to foster church renewal that is both spiritual and practical.

Steinbron, Melvin J. *Can the Pastor Do It Alone? Preparing Lay People for Lay Pastoring.* Ventura, Calif.: Regal, 1987, 258 pages.

A pastor's experience in transitioning from "doing the ministry" to "producing ministers." Offers many helpful insights.

Sullivan, Bill M. *Ten Steps to Breaking the 200 Barrier.* Kansas City, Mo.: Beacon Hill, 1988, 99 pages.

Going beyond a solid theoretical base, and drawing on years of practical experience, the author provides useful how-to-do-it advice applicable to any church currently at "survival size."

Tillapaugh, Frank R. *Unleashing the Church: Getting People out of the Fortress and into Ministry.* Ventura, Calif.: Regal, 1982, 224 pages.

The author challenges churches to forsake the "fortress" mentality, and instead use their spiritual gifts to launch vital, need-meeting ministries in their communities. The book devotes only a small amount of attention to worship, but it lays an essential foundation to the "unleashed" perspective necessary for the development of lay-led worship teams, guilds, troupes, and forums.

Tournier, Paul. *Guilt and Grace.* New York: Harper & Row, 1983, 244 pages.

This is a masterful study of the nature of guilt, its effect on the person, and what the Bible says about transforming guilt into an avenue of God's grace.

Towns, Elmer L. *Ten of Today's Most Innovative Churches: What They're Doing, How They're Doing It and How You Can Apply Their Ideas in Your Church.* Ventura, Calif.: Regal, 1990, 273 pages.

After taking a tour that travels from California to Illinois to Georgia, the author describes five principles that these successful churches have in common.

Towns, Elmer L., John N. Vaughan, and David J. Seifert. *The Complete Book of Church Growth.* Wheaton: Tyndale, 1981, 386 pages.

A thorough textbook that analyzes a number of approaches to church growth. Among its many case studies is a chapter on the role of Fuller Theological Seminary's School of World Mission.

VanVonderen, Jeff. *Tired of Trying to Measure Up: Getting Free from the Demands, Expectations, and Intimidations of Well-Meaning People.* Minneapolis: Bethany House, 1989, 173 pages.

As the subtitle implies, the author, a leading speaker in the Christian recovery movement, starts with the concept of shame and ends with a paradigm of grace.

Vaughan, John N. *The World's 20 Largest Churches: Small Group Church Growth Principles in Action.* Grand Rapids: Baker, 1984, 352 pages.

Identifies the largest churches in the world and surveys the principles by which they have grown. Points out that "every large church began as a small church." Appendices compare memberships, Sunday school attendances, etc.

————. *The Large Church: A Twentieth-Century Expression of the First-Century Church.* Grand Rapids: Baker, 1985, 293 pages.

Analyzes the historic development of the large church, identifies the key issues related to the most common strategies for growth. Gives particular attention to the use of satellite groups.

Wagner, C. Peter. *Leading Your Church to Growth: A Guidebook for Clergy and Laity.* Ventura, Calif.: Regal, 1984, 224 pages.

Addressing both pastors and the congregation, Wagner stresses the fact that strong pastoral leadership and people partnership are essential for dynamic church growth. Dr. Wagner advocates strong pastoral leadership to equip the laity for ministry and shows how this can be developed into a positive growth factor.

————. *Your Church Can Be Healthy.* Nashville: Abingdon, 1979, 120 pages.

A description and analysis of the causes and symptoms of eight major growth-inhibiting diseases found in North American churches.

————. *Your Church Can Grow: Seven Vital Signs of a Healthy Church.* Ventura, Calif.: Regal, 1976, revised 1980, 170 pages.

Wagner's first book on American church growth has now become a basic document in the field. It offers practical insight on how a church can grow.

————. *Your Spiritual Gifts Can Help Your Church Grow.* Ventura, Calif.: Regal, 1979, 272 pages.

This book, one of the most popular on the subject, examines twenty-seven different gifts. The discussions are both objective and practical.

Wardle, Terry Howard. *Exalt Him!* Camp Hill, Pa.: Christian Publications, 1988, 154 pages.

Subtitled *Designing Dynamic Worship Services,* this readable and practical book covers the spectrum from edifying believers to appealing to visitors. A helpful resource for those who desire to release their congregations for a faith-building, encouraging worship experience.

Warren, Rick. *Dynamic Bible Study Methods.* Wheaton: Victor, 1989, 233 pages.

Twelve practical approaches for searching the Scriptures. The author pastors Saddleback Valley Community Church in southern California, which has grown to an attendance of almost 5,000 people.

Webber, Robert E. *Worship Is a Verb.* Waco: Word, 1985, 221 pages.

This book offers many creative solutions to worship as a spectator sport. Among its insights are emphases on the celebrative dimensions of worship, on helpful ways to follow the church year, and on use of the arts in corporate worship.

Westing, Harold J. *Multiple Church Staff Handbook.* Grand Rapids: Kregel, 1985, 208 pages.

A systematic analysis of how team ministry can be enhanced. Well written, practical, filled with illustrations and numerous case studies.

Willard, Dallas, *The Spirit of the Disciplines: Understanding How God Changes Lives.* San Francisco: Harper & Row, 1988, 224 pages.

How the practice of the classic disciplines affirms human life to the fullest. Establishes a foundation for Christian growth.

Williams, Dan. *Seven Myths about Small Groups.* Downers Grove, Ill.: InterVarsity, 1991, 134 pages.

Whether your group wants to get off to a strong start or needs to refocus its vision, here are helpful illustrations, creative ideas, and practical wisdom for growth.

Wimber, John. *Power Evangelism.* New York: Harper & Row, 1986, 224 pages.

The author affirms the reality of miracles in everyday Christian life, linking this to spiritual renewal and the practice of personal evangelism that brings others to faith.

Zunkel, C. Wayne. *Growing the Small Church: A Guide for Church Leaders.* Elgin, Ill.: David C. Cook, 1982, 100 pages.

This is an extremely practical manual with extensive professional artwork for teaching the contents to others. It is much more than theory. If its principles are followed, the prognosis for growth in almost any small church will be good.

Subject Index

(Page references to charts are in italics.)

227

Cunningham, Loren and Darlene, 48
Custodian, 158

Day schools, 63, *65*
Deacons, 118, 159, 166
Delegation and supervision, 23, 90,
    94–95, 137, 159–164, 186–187.
    See also Lay leadership develop-
    ment
Dependency on the pastor, 76, 88–89,
    96–97, 102
Desire to grow, 73–74, 133
Drama, 66
Dysfunctional habits, 118, 152

Eastside Foursquare Church, Kirkland,
    191
Empowerment, 77–80, 107. *See also*
    Lay pastoral skills
Entertainment, role of, 67, 72
Evangelical Free Church, *130–131*
Evangelism, 18, 19, 29, 35–36, 45–46,
    51, 61–63, 76, 80, 87, 98–99, 102,
    163, 170–174, 186, 188, 195–197

Facilities, 51–53, 137–143, *138*, 183
    parking, 137–38
    seating, 51–53, 137, *138*, 139
    property, 139–43
Falwell, Jerry, 66
Fatigue and burnout, 15, 30, 116–118,
    162, 166–167, 173–174
Federal Express, 28, 43
Feeder and receptor patterns, 60–63,
    65, 174, 187
Finances, 30–31, 146, 153–154,
    177–178
First Baptist Church, Dallas, 64
First Baptist Church, Hammond, 64,
    178
First Baptist Church, Modesto, 66
First Evangelical Free Church, Fuller-
    ton, 75–76

God's will, 73–74, 123–24

Governing committee. *See* Boards.
Groups, importance of small-group net-
    work, 19–23, *22*, 67, 94, 106,
    135–137, 169–171, 173, 176–178,
    183–197, *190*. *See also* Lay pas-
    toral skills
Growth
    analogies of
        aspirin, 58–59
        coaching, 79–80
        grapes, 179
        marquee vs. rewiring, 192–193
        McDonald's hamburger chain,
            193, 195–196
        medical team, 13–15, 19
        Pogo, 18
        pre-wiring for crisis, 133
    bias, 71–80
    sources, 28–35, 63–64, *65*, 133;
    misdiagnosed, 59–67
    statistics, 21, 73, 130, *130–131*

Haugk, Kenneth, 185–86
Healing. *See* Miracles; Recovery.
Hero making, 46, 94
Highland Park Baptist Church, 64
Hiring. *See* Staffing issues.
Holy Spirit, 17, 23, 72–73, 102, 106,
    150, 176–177, 184–185, 187, 195
"How to Break the 200 Barrier" sem-
    inar and concepts, 73–74, 129–143
Hunt, Josh, 177
Hybels, Bill, 41–42, 49–50, 51, 66. *See
    also* Willow Creek Community
    Church
Hyles, Jack, 64, 66, 178

Immigration, 64, *65*

Lay leadership development, 178–179,
    180, *194*. *See also* Groups; Spiri-
    tual gifts
Lay pastoral skills, 169–171, 175–176,
    184–189, 192–197, *194*

Scripture Index

Philippians
4:12-13—122

Colossians
1:18—110
2:7—87

1 Timothy
3:2—86

2 Timothy
2:2—196

1 Thessalonians
5:11—87

Titus
1:7—86

Hebrews
2:11—110
11—46
12:2—124
13:7, 17—86

1 Peter
1:3-9—122
4:17—110
5:4—86

Revelation
22:17—110